Knockout

12 Showstopping Neutral Quilts

Neutrals

Pat Wys

Martingale®
Create with Confidence

Dedication

Where there is great love, there are always miracles.   –Willa Cather

We fell in love. We married. *(We were so young.)* We had two amazing daughters. We just celebrated 40 wonderful years. I've been told how lucky I am to have a husband so fabulous. I totally agree, but luck is only part of it. We've enjoyed every moment and lived a life that is, well, epic. We are a team, we are best friends, we are parents, and the love we have is one of a kind!

I married a man who wakes up every morning with only one goal, and that is to make his family happy, safe, and loved. He's selfless, caring, brilliant, and kind, and I'm blessed to walk beside the best husband, friend, and soul mate. On our 40th anniversary we decided we were going to celebrate 40 more years, and I can't wait!

Happy 40th Anniversary, Robert Andrew Wys Jr. This book, and my happy life, happened because of you.

Knockout Neutrals: 12 Showstopping Neutral Quilts
© 2013 by Pat Wys

Martingale®
19021 120th Ave. NE, Ste. 102
Bothell, WA 98011-9511 USA
ShopMartingale.com

Printed in China

18 17 16 15 14 13   8 7 6 5 4 3 2 1

Library of Congress Cataloging-in-Publication Data is available upon request.

ISBN: 978-1-60468-249-6

Mission Statement

Dedicated to providing quality products and service to inspire creativity.

Credits

PRESIDENT AND CEO: Tom Wierzbicki
EDITOR IN CHIEF: Mary V. Green
DESIGN DIRECTOR: Paula Schlosser
MANAGING EDITOR: Karen Costello Soltys
ACQUISITIONS EDITOR: Karen M. Burns
TECHNICAL EDITOR: Ellen Pahl
COPY EDITOR: Sheila Chapman Ryan
PRODUCTION MANAGER: Regina Girard
COVER AND INTERIOR DESIGNER: Connor Chin
PHOTOGRAPHER: Brent Kane
ILLUSTRATOR: Missy Shepler

Special thanks to Pam and Josh Narode for generously allowing us to photograph in their home.

Contents

69

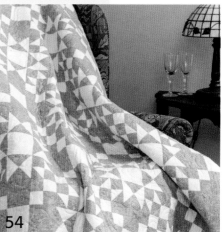

54

22

Introduction

My love of making quilts with neutral fabrics continues. In this sequel to *Spotlight on Neutrals* (Martingale, 2011), I've used more neutrals—and neutral fabrics are even better now! The fabric industry is making neutrals that are prettier and higher quality all the time.

In this book, I overcame my single-minded vision of only using 100% cotton fabric. When I coupled cotton neutrals with other fabrics such as wool, silk, linen, and velvet, I was in quilt designer's heaven. The fabric combinations are endless and so fun to think about and plan. I believe that I'll do more fabric combinations in the future. With color too!

I can't tell you how enjoyable it is to see quilters jumping in and making all-neutral quilts. I hear from people all the time that making a neutral quilt was something they never thought about, but now that they've made one, they'll continue to do so in

the future. Many quilters have told me that their quilting experience and the way they look at different quilt patterns has been broadened significantly through using neutrals. If you like the all-neutral look, wait 'til you see what this second look at neutrals will bring you. Let's get started and play with neutrals. Here we go!

The Value of Value

Since writing *Spotlight on Neutrals*, I've been teaching around the country and showing the quilts from the book. I always ask the group I'm speaking with to tell me what a neutral fabric is to them. I get adjectives such as ugly, drab, guy-quilt fabric, blenders, soft, boring, backgrounds. And then there was this comment: "Whatever matches the rest of the quilt!"

In just about every case I hear people say, "Well, I didn't know gray was neutral. I love gray!" Or, "I never thought of mixing brown with black and gray." I explain to quilting groups that a neutral is anything that's not on the color wheel. Plain and simple. Here's the big news. Get ready. You may need to read this sentence twice! If you want to learn about color, make an all-neutral quilt. Better yet, make a scrappy neutral quilt. Now you're completely confused, right? Let me explain.

My friend Sarah was helping me with some sewing for this book. She said to me, "I learned so much about value and putting fabrics together from those neutral fabrics you gave me to sew with. You should tell people they need to do this!" That's what my lectures, classes, and this book are all about. Have you ever heard the expression "value does the work and color gets the credit"? What Sarah discovered is the total impact of *value*. She learned how to take fabrics with *no color* and put them together to create movement, visual interest, and sparkle. By eliminating the color, all we have to deal with are value and contrast. So the lesson is very eye-opening.

After you experience this, fabric choices and placement in a quilt will be easier when you do use color. You'll see that changes in value (the ratio of dark to light) when strategically planned will make all the difference in the overall look of your finished quilt. Take a look at my quilt "Day and Night" below. It has no color, just black and white—the most extreme example of value. The contrast is easy to see.

Using just black and white in a quilt makes value easy to see.

Now look at "Road Trip" below. This quilt has lots of sparkle because I combined many fabrics—black, brown, tan, very light creams, gray, taupe, you name it. If it's neutral, it's in this quilt. It's the placement of lights right next to darks that makes the fabric jump and move. That strategic placement of value in design, whether you're working with neutrals or colors, is where we get the term *contrast*. Value and contrast are both important in designing quilts. Look at them with a sharper eye. You won't believe what you'll see.

Placing lights next to darks creates contrast.

It really pays to know who you are as a quilter. For example, if you're in love with soft, subtle fabrics and quilts without a lot of visual movement, don't pick fabrics with strong changes in value. Likewise, if you want to focus on one color or several colors but you don't want the quilt blocks to make the strongest statement, choose colors that are very close in value, with *low* contrast.

However, if you like to see the design of the blocks and their secondary pattern, choose fabrics with strong changes in value and stitch them right next to each other. I like most all quilts, but I think you can tell, by the designs in this book, which way I tend to lean. I'll let you figure that out.

The bottom line is this. Learn about value and the creation or elimination of contrast. You will be a more confident shopper when you choose fabrics for a quilt. You won't have to use just one line of fabric either—you'll be grabbing fabric from all over the store. And, if you run out of a fabric in the middle of a project, don't sweat the small stuff. Substitute another fabric of the same value and off you go!

Mist

Not just an ordinary black-and-white quilt, "Mist" features the addition of gray fabrics to soften the overall look of the design. The pieced border adds sparkle and graphic appeal, but admittedly, it takes a lot of half-square triangles! These units make up the bulk of the sewing, so turn on your favorite music or movie and chain sew like crazy.

The distance is nothing. It's only the first step that's important.

–Marquise Du Deffand

Materials

Yardage is based on 42"-wide fabric.

3½ yards of white print for blocks and pieced border

2⅛ yards of black tone-on-tone print for first border, third border, and binding

1¾ yards *total* of assorted black prints for blocks and pieced border

1¾ yards *total* of assorted gray prints for blocks and pieced border

4½ yards of fabric for backing

80" x 80" piece of batting

Cutting

From the white print, cut:
6 strips, 4½" x 42"; crosscut into 48 squares, 4½" x 4½"
25 strips, 3" x 42"; crosscut into 316 squares, 3" x 3"
4 strips, 2½" x 42"; crosscut into 56 squares, 2½" x 2½"

From the assorted black prints, cut:
184 squares, 3" x 3"
50 squares, 2½" x 2½"

From the assorted gray prints, cut:
184 squares, 3" x 3"
50 squares, 2½" x 2½"

From the black tone-on-tone print, cut:
7 strips, 2½" x 42"
8 strips, 3" x 42"
306" of 2½"-wide bias strips for binding

Bigger Is Better

Whenever possible, I like to make oversized units. I don't waste fabric, but give myself the opportunity to square up the units to the perfect size before continuing. My favorite tool for this purpose is a Tucker Trimmer. It's a clean ruler without a lot of intricate measurement lines. It has the 45° angle line that I need for making half-square-triangle units and the added bonus of the opposite 45° angle marked for quarter-square triangles.

Making the Half-Square-Triangle Units

In the following steps, you'll make all of the half-square-triangle units for the A and B blocks and the pieced borders.

1 Pair 158 black 3" squares with 158 white 3" squares, right sides together. Draw a line diagonally from corner to corner on the wrong side of the white squares. Sew ¼" from the drawn line on both sides.

2 Cut the units apart on the drawn line and press the seam allowances toward the black fabric. Square the units to 2½" x 2½". You'll have a total of 316 white/black half-square-triangle units.

Make 316 total.

3 Repeat steps 1 and 2 using 158 gray and 158 white 3" squares to make 316 white/gray half-square-triangle units. Repeat the steps using 26 gray and 26 black 3" squares to make 52 gray/black half-square-triangle units.

Make 316 total.   Make 52 total.

Making Block A

1 Arrange and sew two white 2½" squares, two black/white half-square-triangle units, and two gray/white half-square-triangle units together as shown to make a block row. Press the seam allowances as indicated by the arrows to ensure that you will have opposing seams when you sew the rows together. Make two.

Make 2.

2 Arrange and sew two black/white, two gray/white, and two gray/black half-square-triangle units together as shown to make a block row. Press. Make two.

Make 2.

Pieced by Teresa Wade; quilted by Geraldine Jordan
Finished quilt: 73½" x 73½"
Finished block: 12" x 12"

3 Arrange and sew two black/white half-square-triangle units, two gray/white half-square-triangle units, one black 2½" square, and one gray 2½" square together as shown to make a block row. Press. Make two.

Make 2.

4 Sew the rows together as shown to complete the block. Square up the block to 12½" x 12½". Repeat the steps to make 13 blocks.

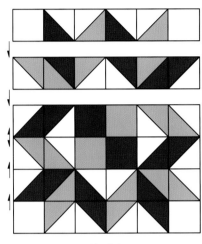

Block A.
Make 13.

Making Block B

1 Draw a line from corner to corner on the wrong side of 24 black 2½" squares and 24 gray 2½" squares.

2 Place a black square from step 1 on the corner of a white 4½" square. Sew on the drawn line. Press the triangle unit toward the outside corner of the white square. Fold the square back and trim the excess fabric, leaving a ¼" seam allowance beyond the stitched line. Press the seam allowances toward the triangle. Make 24. Repeat to make 24 using the marked gray 2½" squares.

Make 24. Make 24.

3 Arrange and sew a black/white unit from step 2 together with two black/white half-square-triangle units,

two gray/white half-square-triangle units, and one black 2½" square as shown. Press the seam allowances as indicated by the arrows. Make two.

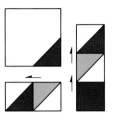 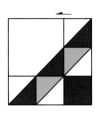

Make 2.

4 Repeat step 3 with a gray/white unit from step 2 and a gray 2½" square.

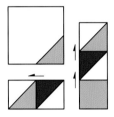 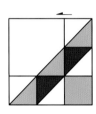

Make 2.

5 Sew the units from steps 3 and 4 together as shown. Square up the block to 12½" x 12½". Repeat all steps to make 12 blocks.

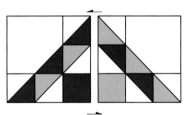

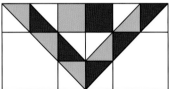

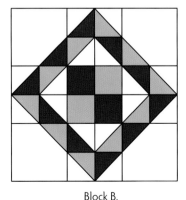

Block B.
Make 12.

Assembling the Quilt Top

1 Arrange the A and B blocks in five horizontal rows of five blocks each, alternating the blocks as shown in the quilt assembly diagram below right. Sew the blocks into rows and press.

2 Sew the rows together and press each long seam open. Your quilt should measure 60½" x 60½".

Speedy Sewing

Check out "Chain Piecing Blocks" on page 75, where I share a technique that I first learned from my friend Sandy. You'll stack all of the blocks at one time and sew them together with speed and accuracy. Give it a try—I promise you'll zip your way to a completed quilt top before you know it. Thanks, Sandy!

3 For the inner border, sew the black tone-on-tone 2½" strips together at 45° angles to make one long strip. Measure the length of the quilt through the center and cut the borders; then sew them to the sides of the quilt center. Press the seam allowances toward the just-added border. Measure the width of the quilt including the borders just added; cut and add the top and bottom borders.

4 For the middle border, use the remaining black/white and gray/white half-square-triangle units. Sew eight of each unit together, alternating them as shown. Press as indicated by the arrows. Repeat to make a second border

strip with the units angled in the opposite direction. Make four of each.

Make 4 of each.

5 Sew one of each strip from step 4 together to make four borders with 32 units in each.

Make 4.

6 Add border strips to the left and right sides of your quilt. Press the seam allowances toward the inner border.

7 Sew a white 2½" square to each end of the two remaining border strips; press the seam allowances toward the white squares. Sew the strips to the top and bottom of your quilt and press the seam allowances toward the inner border.

8 Repeat step 3 to add the black tone-on-tone 3"-wide border strips. Press the seam allowances toward the outer border.

Finishing

For instructions on layering, basting, and quilting, refer to "Finishing School" on page 76. Use the 2½"-wide black tone-on-tone bias strips to make and attach the binding.

Quilt assembly

J'Adore

Quiet elegance is the hallmark of this lovely quilt. Wouldn't *"J'Adore"* (the French expression of adoration) make a beautiful bridal gift? I included a sophisticated taupe silk along with a large-scale print as a focus fabric. With any fabulous fabric, you can transform a bed into something incredible. It will rival any professional decorator's idea of a "statement" bed covering! Stunning is the best description for this quilt.

Pieced by Tricia Wys; quilted by Leisa Wiggley

Finished quilt: 85" x 103"

Finished block: 10" x 10"

Keep your face always toward the sunshine—
and shadows will fall behind you.
–Walt Whitman

Materials

Yardage is based on 42"-wide fabric.

4¾ yards of large-scale light print for blocks and setting triangles

4½ yards of medium-scale light print for sashing units and outer border

3⅝ yards of taupe silk (or quilting cotton) for sashing units and inner border

1 yard of silk fabric (or quilting cotton) for binding

9¼ yards of fabric for backing

93" x 111" piece of batting

8½ yards of iron-on, lightweight woven interfacing (20" wide) for silk

Foundation paper*

*I like Papers for Foundation Piecing from Martingale, but you can use the paper you prefer.

J'Adore Silk!

I used silk fabric to add an extra touch of elegance to this quilt. Don't be afraid to branch out and try it. I recommend that you stabilize the silk with an iron-on, lightweight *woven* interfacing to prevent raveling. Iron the stabilizer to the wrong side of the silk yardage, following the manufacturer's instructions to stabilize the whole piece of fabric, and then cut strips and other pieces just as you would any other fabric—it's super easy!

Other tips for working with silk: don't use pins, use the silk setting on your iron without steam, and dry clean any quilts that contain silk.

Cutting

From the large-scale light print, cut:

11 strips, 10½" x 42"; crosscut into 32 squares, 10½" x 10½"

4 squares, 15½" x 15½"; cut into quarters diagonally to yield 16 triangles (2 are extra)

2 squares, 8" x 8"; cut in half diagonally to yield 4 triangles

From the taupe silk or cotton, cut *on the lengthwise grain*:

2 strips, 2½" x 92"

2 strips, 2½" x 80"

From the remainder of the taupe silk or cotton, cut:

160 rectangles, 3" x 5½"

31 squares, 3" x 3"

5 squares, 3¾" x 3¾"; cut into quarters diagonally to yield 20 triangles (2 are extra)

From the medium-scale light print, cut *on the lengthwise grain*:

2 strips, 6½" x 96"

2 strips, 6½" x 90"

From the remainder of the medium-scale light print, cut:

320 rectangles, 2½" x 4"; cut in half diagonally to yield 640 triangles

124 squares, 1½" x 1½"

From the binding fabric, cut:

475" of 2½"-wide bias binding for scalloped edges

Making the Sashing Units

The rectangular sashing units are paper pieced. They're easy to make, and because you've already cut the triangle corners, they're ready for mass production.

1 Make 160 copies of the pattern on page 16 onto your foundation paper.

2 Place a taupe 3" x 5½" rectangle on the wrong side (unmarked side) of the foundation pattern and pin in place. This is piece 1. Place a medium-scale light triangle right sides together with the taupe rectangle over the space numbered 2 on your pattern. Hold the piece up to the light to make sure that the diagonal edge of the triangle extends ¼" beyond the line between pieces 1 and 2. You can pin the piece in position if desired. With paper side up, stitch along the line using a shorter than normal stitch length (approximately 14 stitches per inch). Remove the unit from the machine and check to make sure the triangle covers space 2. Trim the seam allowance to ¼" and press.

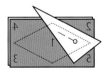 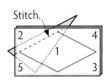

Chain Those Units!

There are a lot of sashing units in this quilt. (I'm sure you figured that out by now.) To speed things up, you can chain piece each triangle corner as you paper piece. Stitch all of the triangles for space 2 at one time and then continue with the triangles for space 3 on the opposite corner. Then trim and press both triangles for all units. You'll certainly save yourself a bunch of time (and thread!) if you work efficiently during these steps. It's not difficult because the paper stabilizes the fabric as you run these babies under the machine.

3 Place a second triangle in the opposite corner, over the space numbered 3, and repeat the process. Do this again for pieces 4 and 5.

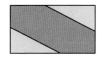 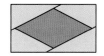

4 After you've finished paper piecing the sashing units and trimming the seam allowances, press and trim the units to 3" x 5½". Remove the paper foundations and press each unit again. Make 160.

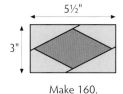

Make 160.

Making the Square-in-a-Square Units

1 Draw a diagonal line from corner to corner on the wrong side of the medium-scale light 1½" squares.

2 Sew marked squares to opposite corners of a taupe 3" square. Press the seam allowances toward the corners; then add squares to the remaining corners. Trim away the bottom two layers of the corners after pressing, leaving a ¼" seam allowance. Make 31 sashing squares.

Make 31.

Check! Check! Check!

I like to check to make sure the triangle corners match up perfectly with the outside corners of the base square before I cut away the bottom two layers. The base square is the exact size of the unfinished unit, so this is an opportunity to check your accuracy and correct any triangle units that aren't aligned properly.

Assembling the Quilt Top

1 Referring to the quilt assembly diagram below, arrange the sashing units, the square-in-a-square units, the taupe triangles, the large-scale print squares, and the large-scale print setting and corner triangles into diagonal rows.

2 Sew the units into diagonal rows, and then sew the rows together. Sew the corner triangles on last.

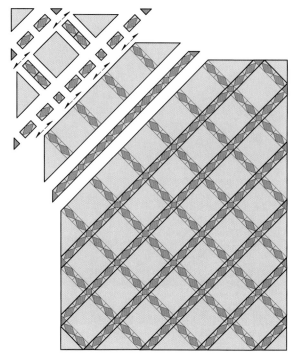

Quilt assembly

3 Measure the length of the quilt top through the center; cut the longer lengths of taupe silk to this measurement and add the side borders. Measure the width of the quilt including the borders just added; cut the shorter strips and add the top and bottom borders. Repeat to add the medium-scale light outer border to the quilt.

Finishing

1 For instructions on layering, basting, and quilting, refer to "Finishing School" on page 76.

2 Quilt as desired and use the 2½"-wide bias strips to make the binding.

3 If you want to scallop the edges of the quilt as shown in the photo, refer to "Scalloping the Outer Border" on page 15. If you don't add scallops, bind your quilt as instructed in "Binding" on page 77. I used silk for the binding, but you can use cotton if you prefer. I did not use interfacing on the silk for binding.

Scalloping the Outer Border

Scallops are marked *after* your quilt has been quilted.

1 Mark the center of each side of the quilt.

2 Mark a guideline on your quilt, parallel to the seam between the inner and outer borders, and about 4" from the seam line.

3 Mark a 45° line on each corner of the quilt.

4 Using the patterns on page 16, make scallop templates in all three sizes. Draw scallops onto the border, beginning with one 10" scallop on each side of the center mark and one scallop at each corner. Trace the scallops across each side using different lengths as needed to fit the length of the quilt. Any difference in size will not be noticeable. For the corners, I used the 10" scallop on each side of the diagonal line, adjusting it as needed for a smooth curve.

Marking scallops

Practice Time!

You may want to use a long length of freezer paper to make a "sample" of what your scallops will look like. This is helpful if you've never scalloped a quilt before. Don't be afraid—it's really quite easy.

5 Sew the bias binding to the quilt, with the raw edges of the binding along the drawn line on the front of the quilt. The folded edge of the binding should be toward the inside of the quilt. Sew and ease the binding into the V of the scallops. Once you have your binding sewn on the line, join the beginning and ending of the binding (see page 78).

Begin sewing.

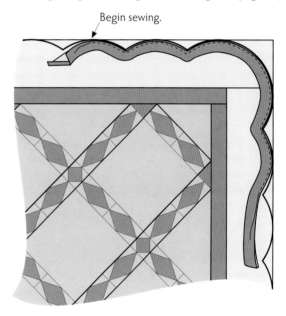

6 Trim the edges of the quilt along the raw edge of the binding and hand stitch the binding to the back. Clip the quilt and binding a tiny bit into each point of the V in the binding. This will help as you hand sew the inside curves of the binding. Don't be timid; go ahead and give it a clip!

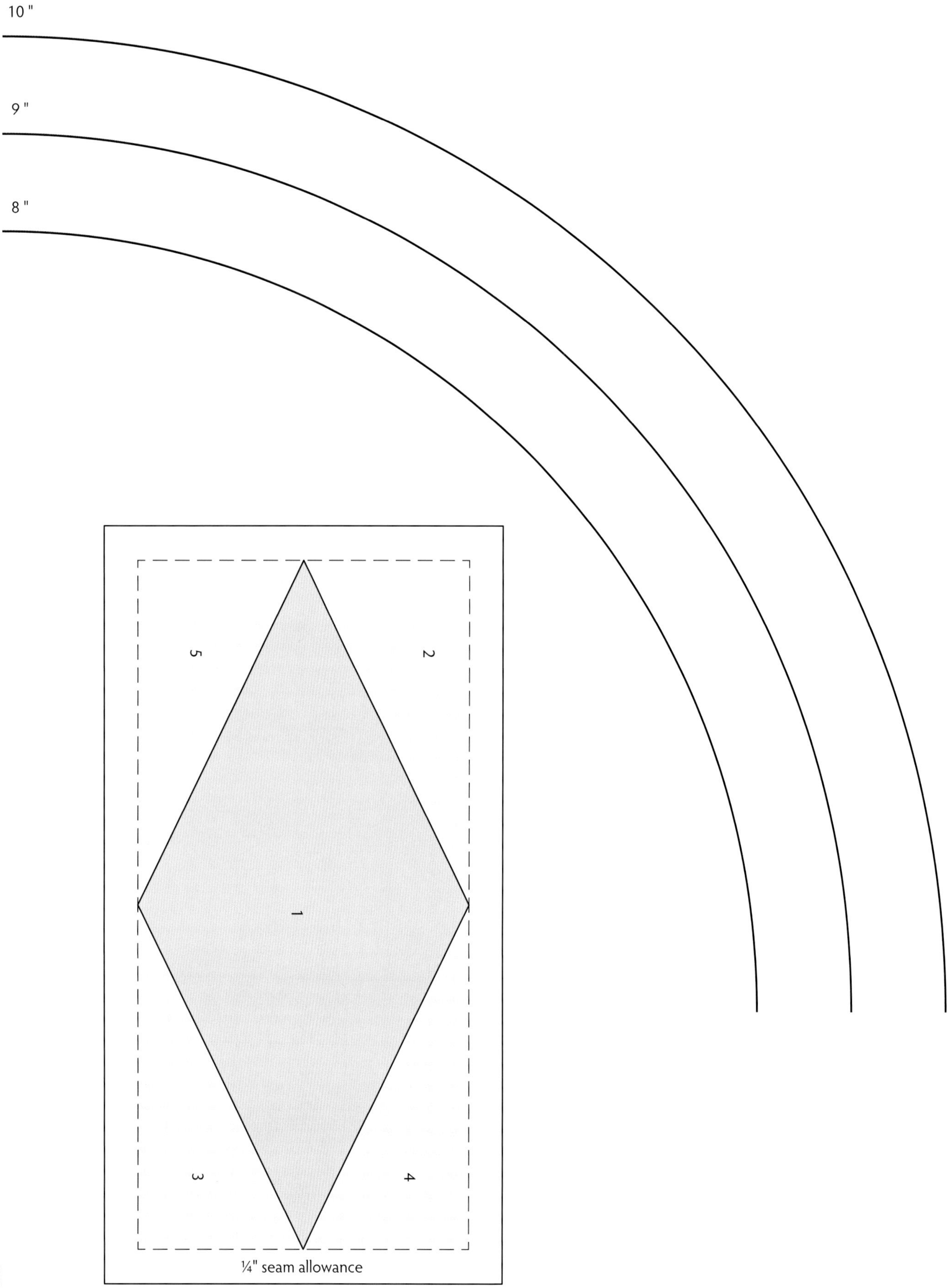

10 "

9 "

8 "

¼" seam allowance

1

2

3

4

5

Day and Night

Opposites attract in this easy-to-construct quilt. For graphic appeal, you can't beat black and white. It is a classic neutral combination that appeals to a wide audience, and there are always plenty of black-and-white fabrics on the market. Fabric substitutions are a breeze! You'll get lots of compliments when you show "Day and Night" off to your friends. You may even need to make more than one!

Pieced by Teresa Wade; quilted by Leisa Wiggley
Finished quilt: 77" x 96"
Finished block: 12" x 12"

Day and Night

Imagination is the true magic carpet.
—Norman Vincent Peale

Materials

Yardage is based on 42"-wide fabric.

3⅛ yards of black solid for blocks, sashing, and setting triangles

3 yards of white solid for blocks, sashing, and setting triangles

1⅞ yards *total* of assorted white prints for blocks and setting triangles

1⅞ yards *total* of assorted black prints for blocks and setting triangles

1 yard of fabric for binding

7 yards of fabric for backing

85" x 104" piece of batting

Cutting

From the white solid, cut:

13 strips, 3½" x 42"; crosscut into 142 squares, 3½" x 3½"

14 strips, 2½" x 42"; crosscut into:
    40 rectangles, 2½" x 6½"
    100 squares, 2½" x 2½"

3 strips, 2" x 42"; crosscut into 49 squares, 2" x 2"

2 strips, 5½" x 42"; crosscut into 9 squares, 5½" x 5½". Cut into quarters diagonally to yield 36 triangles.

From the black solid, cut:

1 strip, 9¾" x 42"; crosscut into 4 squares, 9¾" x 9¾". Cut into quarters diagonally to yield 16 triangles (2 are extra).

12 strips, 2½" x 42"; crosscut into:
    24 rectangles, 2½" x 6½"
    124 squares, 2½" x 2½"

27 strips, 2" x 42"; crosscut into 80 rectangles, 2" x 12½"

2 squares, 5⅛" x 5⅛"; cut in half diagonally to yield 4 triangles

From the assorted white prints, cut:

320 rectangles, 2" x 3½"

From the assorted black prints, cut:

320 rectangles, 2" x 3½"

From the binding fabric, cut:

360" of 2½"-wide bias binding

Making the Blocks

1 Draw a line from corner to corner on the wrong side of 80 black solid and 48 white solid 2½" squares.

2 Place a marked white square on each end of a black 2½" x 6½" rectangle. Sew on the marked lines and press the squares toward the outside corners of the rectangle. Check for accuracy as instructed in "Check Point" below, and then trim the excess fabric at the corners.

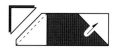

Check Point

After you have sewn the square units onto the base rectangles and pressed the triangles toward the corners, flip the unit over and make sure that the edges of the sewn squares meet up exactly with the edges of the rectangle. If they're a bit over or under you might want to resew the unit. The rectangle is the accurate measurement and the corner squares/triangles should align perfectly.

3 Repeat step 2 to make 24 units with black rectangles and 40 units with white rectangles.

Make 24.   Make 40.

4 Sew black solid and white solid 2½" squares together in groups of three as shown to make 20 units with a black center square and 12 units with a white center square. Press the seam allowances toward the black squares.

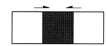

Make 20.   Make 12.

5 Sew the units from steps 3 and 4 together to make the block centers as shown.

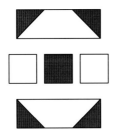

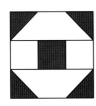 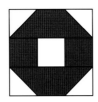

Make 20. Make 12.

6 Sew white and black 2" x 3½" rectangles together to make 320 rectangle pairs. Press the seam allowances toward the black rectangles. Sew the pairs together as shown to make 160 units. Press. The units should measure 3½" x 6½".

Make 320. Make 160.

Why Did I Do That?

You may be wondering why I cut the print fabrics into 2" x 3½" rectangles. Why didn't I just sew the 42" strips of fabric together to make a strip set, and then crosscut the rectangles? Well, I did it for three reasons. First, I like to "shuffle the deck" with a wide variety of fabric combinations. By cutting the fabric into smaller rectangles, I could do that. Second, sewing accuracy is improved if you're not spanning the entire crosswise length of a fabric strip as you sew. Third, I like "mindless" sewing and chain piecing so that I can easily watch a movie while I sew, or chat it up with my sewing friends!

7 Sew a white 3½" square to each end of 64 units from step 6. Press the seam allowances toward the white squares.

Make 64.

8 Sew units from step 6 to the left and right sides of each block center. Press the seam allowances toward the center square.

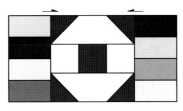

Make 20.

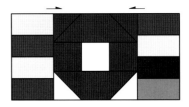

Make 12.

9 Sew units from step 7 to the top and bottom of the units from step 8. Press the seam allowances open. The blocks should measure 12½" x 12½". Make 20 blocks with a black center square and 12 blocks with a white center square.

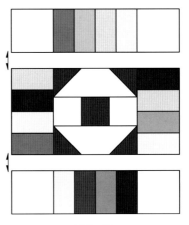

Make 20.

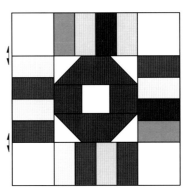

Make 12.

Making the Setting Triangles

1 Sew two units from step 6 of "Making the Blocks" together with one black 9¾" triangle, two white 5½" triangles, and one white 3½" square as shown. Press. Make 14 side setting triangle units.

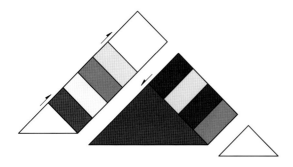

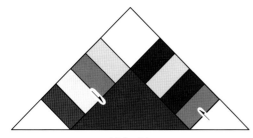

Make 14.

2 Sew one step 6 unit, one black 5⅛" triangle, and two white 5½" triangles together as shown. Press. Make four corner setting triangle units.

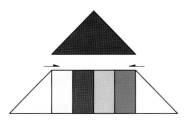

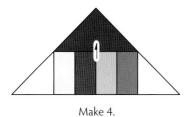

Make 4.

Assembling the Quilt Top

1 Referring to the quilt assembly diagram below, arrange the blocks, black sashing strips, white sashing squares, and setting triangles into diagonal rows.

2 Sew the block rows and sashing rows as shown. Then sew the rows together to complete your quilt top. Trim the white squares along the edges. The setting triangles are all the borders you need for this terrific quilt.

Quilt assembly

Finishing

For instructions on layering, basting, and quilting, refer to "Finishing School" on page 76. Use the 2½"-wide bias strips to make and attach the binding.

Arboretum

The arboretum in Asheville, North Carolina, is a wonderful, secluded place in the Great Smoky Mountains. My family will always hold this peaceful spot in our hearts and be grateful to have such a beautiful setting to say good-bye to one little angel, gone too soon. In memoriam, Jackson Neil DeLoach, May 7, 2012.

She stood in the storm, and when the wind did not blow her away, she adjusted her sails.
—Elizabeth Edwards

Materials

Yardage is based on 42"-wide fabric.

6½ yards of white print for blocks, setting pieces, and borders

3 yards *total* of assorted light, medium, and dark neutrals for blocks and borders

¼ yard or 1 fat eighth *each* of 3 assorted dark prints for large Tree blocks (tree trunks)

⅛ yard or 1 fat eighth *each* of 15 assorted dark prints for small Tree blocks (tree trunks)

⅞ yard of fabric for binding*

5½ yards of fabric for backing

77" x 96" piece of batting

Foundation paper**

Optional; the quilt shown uses scraps for the binding.

**I like Papers for Foundation Piecing from Martingale, but you can use the paper you prefer.*

Cutting

From the assorted light, medium, and dark fabrics, cut *a total of:*

168 squares, 3" x 3"

9 squares, 2⅞" x 2⅞"; cut in half diagonally to yield 18 triangles

21 squares, 2½" x 2½"*

390 squares, 2" x 2"

45 squares, 1⅞" x 1⅞"; cut in half diagonally to yield 90 triangles

105 squares, 1½" x 1½"*

I cut these squares mainly from dark-value fabrics.

From *each* of the 3 dark prints for large tree trunks, cut:

1 square, 6⅞" x 6⅞"; cut in half diagonally to yield 2 triangles (1 is extra)

1 square, 4" x 4"; cut in half diagonally to yield 2 triangles

1 rectangle, 3½" x 9½"

From *each* of the 15 dark prints for small tree trunks, cut:

1 square, 3⅞" x 3⅞"; cut in half diagonally to yield 2 triangles (1 is extra)

1 square, 2½" x 2½"; cut in half diagonally to yield 2 triangles

1 rectangle, 2" x 5"

From the white print, cut *on the lengthwise grain:*

2 strips, 3" x 79½"

2 strips, 3" x 69½"

1 strip, 2" x 51½"

4 squares, 20" x 20"; cut into quarters diagonally to yield 16 triangles (2 are extra)

From the remainder of the white print, cut:

2 strips, 3⅝" x 42"; crosscut into 6 rectangles, 3⅝" x 9½"

2 strips, 6⅞" x 42"; crosscut into 8 squares, 6⅞" x 6⅞". Cut in half diagonally to yield 16 triangles (1 is extra).

4 strips, 2" x 42"; crosscut into 30 rectangles, 2" x 5"

4 strips, 3⅞" x 42"; crosscut into 38 squares, 3⅞" x 3⅞". Cut in half diagonally to yield 76 triangles (1 is extra).

2 squares, 12" x 12"; cut in half diagonally to yield 4 triangles

1 square, 11" x 11"

2 strips, 9½" x 42"; crosscut into:
   3 rectangles, 9½" x 12½"
   1 rectangle, 9½" x 11"

7 strips, 2" x 42"; crosscut into:
   1 strip, 2" x 41"
   1 strip, 2" x 30½"
   1 strip, 2" x 21½"
   2 strips, 2" x 20"
   9 rectangles, 2" x 9½"

6 strips, 1¼" x 42"; crosscut into:
   6 strips, 1¼" x 18½"
   6 strips, 1¼" x 20"

3 strips, 2½" x 42"; crosscut into:
   1 rectangle, 2½" x 10"
   2 rectangles, 2½" x 9"
   1 rectangle, 2½" x 8½"
   1 rectangle, 2½" x 8"
   3 rectangles, 2½" x 6½"
   2 rectangles, 2½" x 6"
   4 rectangles, 2½" x 5½"
   2 rectangles, 2½" x 4"

From the binding fabric or scraps, cut:

330" of 2½"-wide bias strips

Pieced by Debbie Frey; quilted by Leisa Wiggley
Finished quilt: 69½" x 88½"
Finished blocks: 18" x 18" and 9" x 9"

Making the Half-Square-Triangle Units

You'll make all of the half-square-triangle units for the blocks and borders first.

1 Pair assorted light and medium 3" squares with medium or dark 3" squares to make 168 half-square-triangle units for the large trees and pieced borders. Square up the units to 2½" x 2½".

Make 168.

2 Pair assorted light and medium 2" squares with medium or dark 2" squares to make 390 half-square-triangle units for the small trees. Square up the units to 1½" x 1½".

Make 390.

Making the Blocks

You'll make the large and small Tree blocks in the same manner: first making the trunk section, and then the tree tops.

Tree Trunks

1 Make three copies of the patterns for the large Tree block on pages 31 and 32 onto your foundation paper.

2 Begin with the white 3⅝" x 9½" rectangles and a dark 4" triangle. Place the white rectangle right side up on the wrong side of piece 1 in section 1. Pin in place and add the dark triangle, right sides together with the rectangle. Hold the piece up to the light to make sure that at least ¼" of the dark triangle extends beyond the diagonal line between pieces 1 and 2.

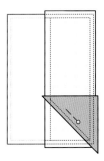

3 With the paper side up and using a shorter than normal stitch length (approximately 14 stitches per inch), sew along the diagonal line. Trim the seam allowance to ¼" and press the triangle toward the corner.

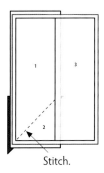 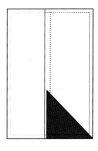

Stitch.

4 Place a matching dark 3½" x 9½" rectangle right sides together on pieces 1 and 2. With the paper side up, stitch on the line; press it over space 3.

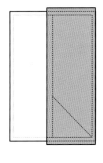 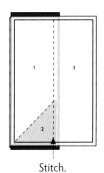

Stitch.

5 Piece the second section of the pattern in the same manner using a second white print 3⅝" x 9½" rectangle for piece 4 and a matching dark 4" triangle for piece 5.

6 Sew the sections together. Press the seam allowances toward the trunk and trim the edges of the unit along the outer lines. Gently remove the foundation paper and press again.

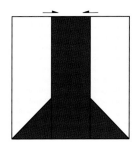

7 Sew a matching dark 6⅞" triangle to the top of the tree-trunk unit. Sew a white 6⅞" triangle to the bottom of each trunk. Press the seam allowances away from the center.

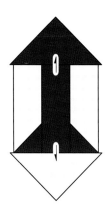

8 Sew white 6⅞" triangles to the left and right sides of the trunk unit. The unit should measure 12½" square. Repeat the steps to make three large tree-trunk sections (unit A).

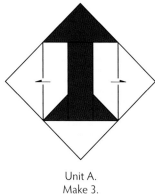

Unit A.
Make 3.

9 Make 15 copies of the patterns for the small Tree blocks on page 32. Repeat steps 2–8 to make 15 small tree-trunk sections. Use the following pieces for each Tree block: two white 2" x 5" rectangles for pieces 1 and 4, two dark 2½" triangles for pieces 2 and 5, one dark 2" x 5" rectangle for piece 3, one dark 3⅞" triangle, and three white print 3⅞" triangles. The finished units should measure 6½" square.

Tree Tops

1 Arrange three assorted 2½" half-square-triangle units in rows together with three assorted 2⅞" triangles. Sew the units into rows and press. Sew the rows together. Make six units.

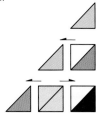

Make 6.

2 Sew a white 6⅞" triangle to the diagonal side of each triangle unit from step 1; this is unit B. Make six. The units will measure 6½" x 6½".

Unit B.
Make 6.

3 Arrange and sew together two assorted dark 2½" squares and seven scrappy half-square-triangle units as shown. Make three of each unit. These units are identical with one important exception—the angles of the half-square triangles are different. These are units C and D. The units will measure 6½" x 6½". Press the seam allowances as indicated by the arrows.

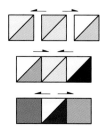

Unit C.
Make 3.

Unit D.
Make 3.

4 Arrange and sew together three dark 2½" squares and six half-square-triangle units as shown. Place the dark squares so that there's a chain of unpieced squares running diagonally through the middle of the block. Press. This is unit E. The units will measure 6½" x 6½".

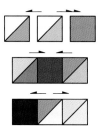

Unit E.
Make 3.

5 Repeat steps 1–4 to make units for 15 small Tree blocks. Use the assorted 1½" half-square-triangle units, the remaining white 3⅞" triangles, the dark 1⅞" squares, and the dark 1½" squares. The finished units will measure 3½" square. Make 30 of unit B, and 15 each of units C, D, and E.

Joining Tree Tops and Trunks

1 Arrange one B unit with units C and E in a row as shown, and then sew them together. Press the seam allowances as shown by the arrows. Join unit D with the second B unit and press; stitch these to the side of the tree-trunk unit (A) as shown. Join the two rows and press. The block should measure 18½" square. Make three large Tree blocks.

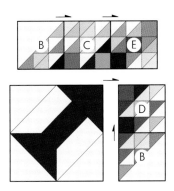

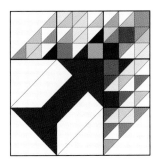

Make 3.

2 Repeat step 1 using the 3½" units and the 6½" tree-trunk units. Make 15 small Tree blocks. The blocks should measure 9½" square.

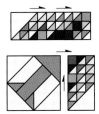

Make 15.

Making the Corner Units

Assemble four corner units for the quilt as shown by first sewing a white 2" x 9½" rectangle to one side of each of four small Tree blocks. Note the orientation of the blocks and the placement of the strips; you'll sew the strip to a *different side* of each block. Sew white 20" triangles to two sides of each of the four blocks. Add a white 12" triangle to each unit. Note that the triangles are cut oversized. This will give the Tree blocks space to "float" in the center of the quilt.

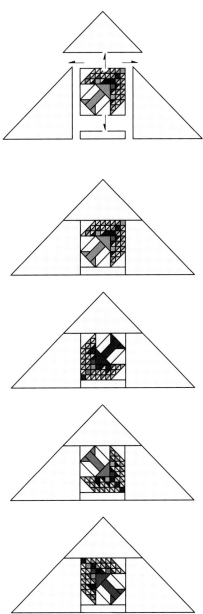

Make 1 of each.

Assembling the Quilt Top

Press all seam allowances away from the Tree blocks.

1 Sew white 1 1/4" x 18 1/2" strips to the left and right sides of each large Tree block. Sew white 1 1/4" x 20" strips to the top and bottom. Press.

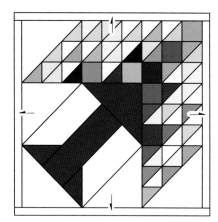

2 Make diagonal row 1 by sewing two small Tree blocks, a white 9 1/2" x 12 1/2" rectangle, a white 2" x 30 1/2" strip, and two white 20" triangles together as shown.

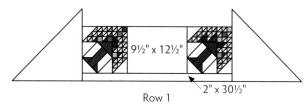

9 1/2" x 12 1/2"

2" x 30 1/2"

Row 1

3 Make diagonal row 2 in sections. To make section 1, sew two large Tree blocks together with a white 2" x 20" strip between them. Add the white 2" x 41" strip to the bottom of the section.

2" x 20"

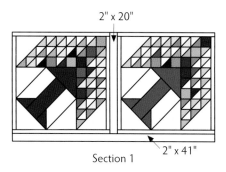

2" x 41"

Section 1

4 Make section 2 of row 2 by sewing two small Tree blocks together with a white 2" x 9 1/2" strip between them. Add a white 2" x 9 1/2" strip to the bottom, and then add the white 2" x 21 1/2" strip to the side of the block unit.

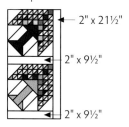

← 2" x 21 1/2"

← 2" x 9 1/2"

← 2" x 9 1/2"

Section 2

5 Make section 3 of row 2 by sewing one white 20" triangle to the top of a white 11" square.

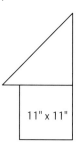

11" x 11"

Section 3

6 Sew the three sections of row 2 together. This is the longest row—it's all downhill from here! Sew row 2 to row 1.

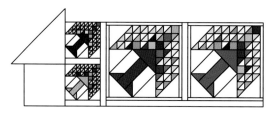

Row 2

7 Row 3 is simple! Sew together four small Tree blocks, the remaining two white 9 1/2" x 12 1/2" rectangles, and a white 2" x 9 1/2" strip as shown. Sew row 3 to row 2.

2" x 9 1/2"

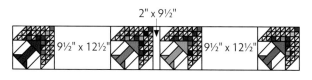

9 1/2" x 12 1/2"   9 1/2" x 12 1/2"

Row 3

8 Row 4 will be sewn in sections. To make section 1, sew a white 2" x 9 1/2" strip to the right side of a small Tree block as shown in step 11 on page 29. Add a white 20" triangle to the bottom.

9 To make section 2, sew a small Tree block to the white 9 1/2" x 11" rectangle. Sew the remaining white 2" x 20" strip to the right side of a large Tree block. Then add the small Tree and rectangle unit to the right side of the strip.

10 To make section 3, sew the remaining white 2" x 9½" strip to the left side of a small Tree block. Add a white 20" triangle to the bottom.

11 Sew sections 1–3 of row 4 together. Sew the 2" x 51½" strip to the top, and then add a white 20" triangle to the end to complete row 4.

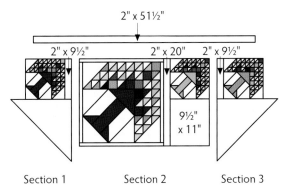

Section 1   Section 2   Section 3

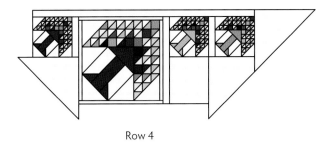

Row 4

12 Sew row 4 to row 3. Add the corner units to each corner. Trim the quilt top so that it measures 60½" x 75½".

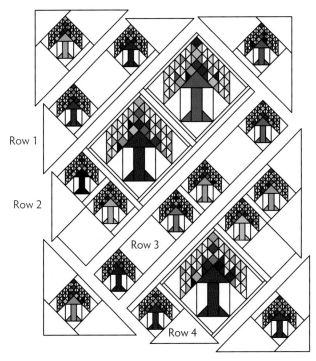

Quilt assembly

Adding the Borders

1 Sew the left side border in the following order from top to bottom (left to right in the diagram). Sew a white 2½" x 4" piece to seven half-square-triangle units. Add a white 2½" x 6½" piece and nine half-square-triangle units. Add a white 2½" x 9" strip, 10 half-square-triangle units, and a white 2½" x 5½" piece. Sew the strip to the left side of the quilt with the triangles pointing away from the quilt center. Press the seam allowances toward the quilt center.

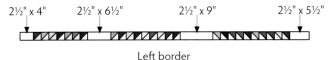

Left border

2 Sew the right side border in the following order from top to bottom (left to right in the diagram). Sew the white 2½" x 8" piece to 12 half-square-triangle units. Add the white 2½" x 8½" strip and four half-square-triangle units. Add a white 2½" x 6" piece, eight half-square-triangle units, and a white 2½" x 6½" piece. Sew the strip to the right side of the quilt with the triangles pointing away from the quilt center. Press the seam allowances toward the quilt center.

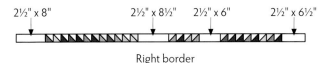

Right border

3 Sew the pieces for the top border in the following order from left to right. Sew a white 2½" x 5½" piece to nine half-square-triangle units. Add the white 2½" x 10" strip and seven half-square-triangle units. Add a white 2½" x 6½" piece, four half-square-triangle units, and a white 2½" x 4" piece. Sew the strip to the top of the quilt. Press the seam allowances toward the quilt center.

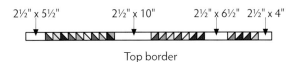

Top border

4 Sew the bottom border in the following order from left to right. Sew a white 2½" x 5½" piece to eight half-square-triangle units. Add a white 2½" x 9" strip and three half-square-triangle units. Add a white 2½" x 6" strip, nine half-square-triangle units, and a white 2½" x 5½" piece. Sew the strip to the bottom of the quilt. Press the seam allowances toward the quilt center.

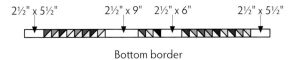

Bottom border

5 Sew the white 3" x 79½" borders to the sides of the quilt. Press the seam allowances toward the outer border. Sew the white 3" x 69½" borders to the top and bottom of the quilt. Press.

Finishing

For instructions on layering, basting, and quilting, refer to "Finishing School" on page 76. After quilting, you may want to add a scrappy binding. A scrappy binding really is the final exclamation point on this lovely quilt! You can also use 2½"-wide bias strips of one fabric to make and attach the binding.

Adding borders

 What is a friend? A single soul dwelling in two bodies.

—Aristotle

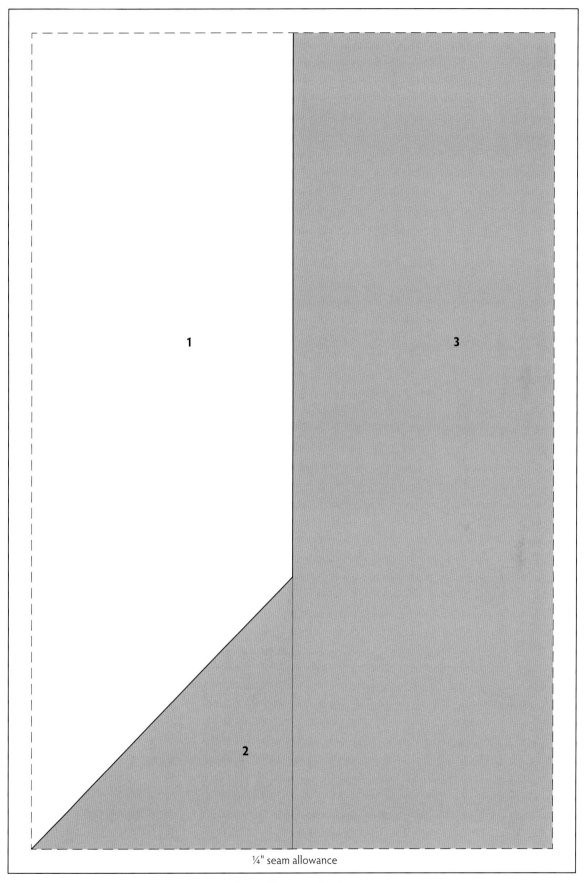

1

3

2

¼" seam allowance

Large Tree section 1

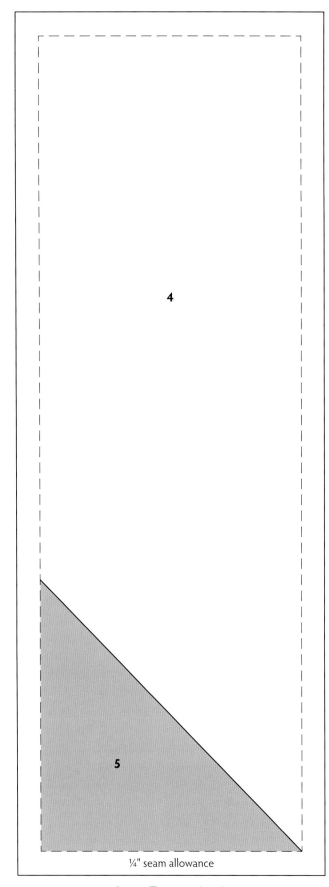

¼" seam allowance

Large Tree section 2

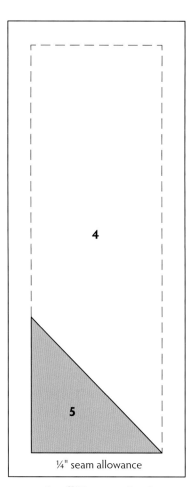

¼" seam allowance

Small Tree section 2

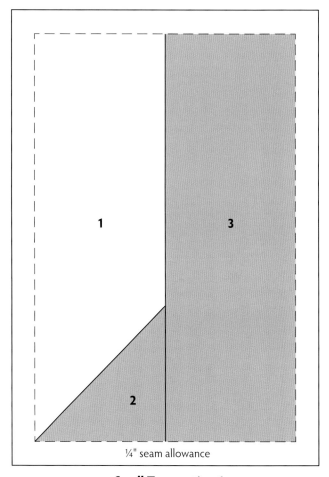

¼" seam allowance

Small Tree section 1

Road Trip

What could be better than a road trip? A road trip with terrific quilting friends! I can hear the chatter now: "Which way are we going?" "Let's have some chocolate!" "Where is the GPS?" "RECALCULATING!" "How much money did you spend?" This quilt reminds me of some of the great trips I've taken with friends. Come with me on a quilty road trip.

Pieced by Marty Miller; quilted by Leisa Wiggley
Finished quilt: 65½" x 81½"
Finished block: 10" x 10"

A journey of a thousand miles begins with a single step.

—Chinese Proverb

Materials

Yardage is based on 42"- wide fabric.

2¾ yards *total* of assorted dark neutral prints for blocks and setting triangles

1¾ yards *total* of assorted medium neutral prints for blocks and setting triangles

1⅔ yards of white print for sashing

1½ yards *total* of assorted light neutral prints for blocks and setting triangles

1¼ yards *total* of assorted black tone-on-tone prints for blocks, sashing cornerstones, and setting triangles

⅞ yard of fabric for binding*

5 yards of fabric for backing

73" x 89" piece of batting

Optional; the quilt shown uses black scraps for the binding.

Cutting

From the assorted light prints, cut *a total of:*
284 squares, 2½" x 2½"

From the assorted dark prints, cut *a total of:*
142 squares, 4½" x 4½"

From the assorted medium prints, cut *a total of:*
320 squares, 2½" x 2½"

From the assorted black tone-on-tone prints, cut *a total of:*
32 squares, 2½" x 2½"

9 squares, 7" x 7"; cut into quarters diagonally to yield 36 triangles

4 squares, 4⅛" x 4⅛"; cut into quarters diagonally to yield 16 triangles (2 are extra)

2 squares, 2⅜" x 2⅜"; cut in half diagonally to yield 4 triangles

49 squares, 2" x 2"

From the white print, cut:
21 strips, 2" x 42"; crosscut into 80 rectangles, 2" x 10½"

From the binding fabric, cut:
306" of 2½"-wide bias strips

Making the Blocks and Setting Triangles

1 Draw a diagonal line from corner to corner on the wrong side of the light 2½" squares.

2 Place two marked light 2½" squares on opposite corners of a dark 4½" square. Stitch on the drawn lines. Press the triangle corners toward the outside edges of the large square. Check to make sure your triangle corners line up precisely with the edges of the larger square, and then trim away the bottom two layers of the triangle corners, leaving a ¼" seam allowance. Make 142.

Make 142.

3 Sew two medium 2½" squares together to make a pair. Make 160 pairs.

Make 160.

4 Arrange four units from step 2 and four pairs from step 3 together in three rows with a black tone-on-tone 2½" square as shown. Sew the units into rows. Press the seam allowances as indicated by the arrows. Sew the rows together. Make 32 blocks.

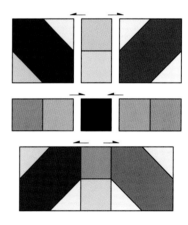

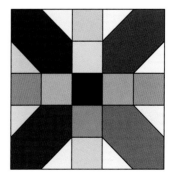

Make 32.

5 Arrange two pairs from step 3 together with one unit from step 2, two black tone-on-tone 7" triangles, and one black tone-on-tone 4⅛" triangle as shown. Sew the units together in rows, pressing the seam allowances as indicated. Sew the rows together. Make 14 pieced side setting triangles.

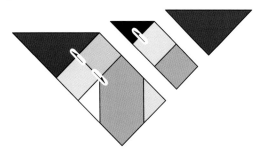

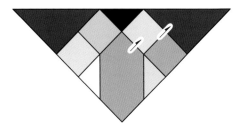

Make 14.

6 Arrange a pair from step 3 together with two black tone-on-tone 7" triangles and one black tone-on-tone 2⅜" triangle as shown. Sew the larger black triangles to the left and right sides of the squares. Press the seam allowances toward the triangles. Then add the smaller black triangle and press. Make four corner setting triangles.

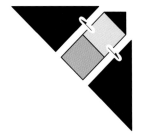

Make 4.

Make Use of the Waste

If you like to make small quilts, you can make bonus half-square-triangle units when sewing the small squares to the corners of the larger squares. Simply sew another line of stitching ½" from the first stitched line. Cut between the two stitched lines and press the seam allowances toward the darker fabric.

Assembling the Quilt Top

1 Referring to the quilt assembly diagram below, arrange the blocks, sashing strips, and sashing squares in diagonal rows. Sew the block and sashing rows, including the side setting triangles, as shown. Join the rows. Press the seam allowances toward the sashing.

2 Add the corner triangles to the quilt. Press the seam allowances toward the sashing.

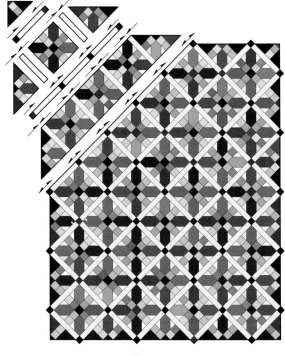

Quilt assembly

3 Trim the sashing squares along the edges of the quilt and square up the corners.

Finishing

For instructions on layering, basting, and quilting, refer to "Finishing School" on page 76. After quilting, you may want to add a scrappy binding. A scrappy binding really is the finishing touch on this beautiful quilt! You can also use 2½"-wide bias strips of one fabric to make and attach the binding.

Dominoes

These "dominoes" are black and white, with a touch of gray—what's more neutral than that? I love the way this quilt shimmers and seems to pulsate as the values change across the surface. The classic granny square gets a modern, up-to-date touch when we play dominoes with fabric. Let's play on!

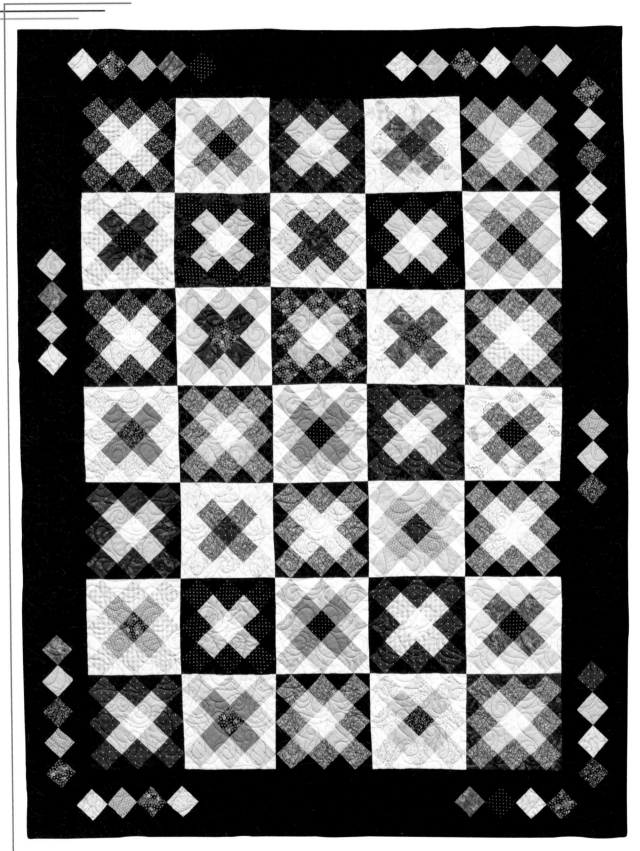

Pieced by Karin Efman; quilted by Leisa Wiggley

Finished quilt: 54" x 71"

Finished block: 8½" x 8½"

To keep a lamp burning, we have to keep putting oil in it.

–Mother Teresa

Materials

Yardage is based on 42"-wide fabric.

3 yards of black tone-on-tone print for blocks, borders, and binding

1¼ yards *total* of assorted light neutral prints for blocks and pieced border

1¼ yards *total* of assorted medium neutral prints for blocks and pieced border

1 yard *total* of assorted white tone-on-tone prints for blocks and pieced border

¼ yard *total* of assorted dark neutral prints for blocks and pieced border

3½ yards of fabric for backing

62" x 79" piece of batting

12" or 14" square ruler

Cutting

From the black tone-on-tone print, cut:

3 strips, 2½" x 42"; crosscut into 36 squares, 2½" x 2½". Cut in half diagonally to yield 72 triangles.*

4 strips, 4¼" x 42"; crosscut into 36 squares, 4¼" x 4¼". Cut into quarters diagonally to yield 144 triangles.*

12 strips, 2" x 42"

4 strips, 3" x 42"; crosscut into:
- 1 strip, 3" x 26"
- 1 strip, 3" x 25½"
- 1 strip, 3" x 18½"
- 1 strip, 3" x 18"
- 2 strips, 3" x 15½"
- 4 squares, 3" x 3"

3 strips, 3¾" x 42"; crosscut into 25 squares, 3¾" x 3¾". Cut into quarters diagonally to yield 100 triangles (2 are extra).

266" of 2½"-wide bias binding

Keep the half-square triangles together for the block corners; keep the quarter-square triangles together for the block sides.

From the assorted white tone-on-tone prints, cut:

18 squares, 2½" x 2½"

17 *matching sets* of:
- 2 squares, 2½" x 2½" (34 total); cut in half diagonally to yield 4 triangles (68 total)
- 2 squares, 4¼" x 4¼" (34 total); cut into quarters diagonally to yield 8 triangles (136 total)

10 squares, 2¼" x 2¼"

From the assorted light prints, cut:

18 *sets of 4 matching* squares, 2½" x 2½" (72 total)

17 *sets of 8 matching* squares, 2½" x 2½" (136 total)

10 squares, 2¼" x 2¼"

From the assorted medium prints, cut:

18 *sets of 8 matching* squares, 2½" x 2½" (144 total)

17 *sets of 4 matching* squares, 2½" x 2½" (68 total)

10 squares, 2¼" x 2¼"

From the assorted dark prints, cut:

17 squares, 2½" x 2½"

10 squares, 2¼" x 2¼"

Making the Blocks

You'll need 18 blocks with a white tone-on-tone center and 17 blocks with a dark center. Each block is made up of four fabrics: a white print, light print, medium print, and dark print.

1 To make the dark-background block, choose one white print 2½" square, four matching light 2½" squares, eight matching medium 2½" squares, eight black tone-on-tone 4¼" triangles, and four black tone-on-tone 2½" triangles. Arrange the squares and triangles in diagonal rows as shown.

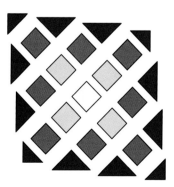

2 Sew the squares and triangles in rows. Press the seam allowances in opposite directions from row to row. Sew the rows together. Note that the triangles are cut slightly oversized; you'll trim the blocks later. Make a total of 18 dark-background blocks.

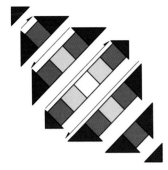

Make 18.

3 To make the light-background blocks, choose one dark 2½" square, four matching medium 2½" squares, eight matching light 2½" squares, and a matching set of eight white tone-on-tone 4¼" triangles and four 2½" triangles. Arrange the squares and triangles in diagonal rows and sew the blocks together as you did before. Make a total of 17 light-background blocks.

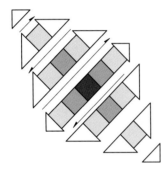
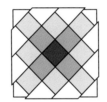

Make 17.

4 Press the blocks carefully and square them up by trimming them with your square ruler and rotary cutter. Lay a square ruler over the block. Make sure you leave ¼" seam allowance beyond the points of the squares. Square the blocks to 9" x 9".

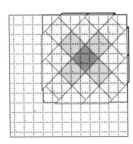
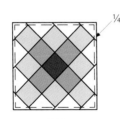
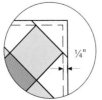

Assembling the Quilt Top

1 Arrange the blocks in seven horizontal rows of five blocks each. Rows 1, 3, 5, and 7 begin and end with a dark-background block. Rows 2, 4, and 6 begin and end with a light-background block. See "Chain Piecing Blocks" on page 75 to stack and sew the quilt top in one sitting. The quilt center should now measure 43" x 60".

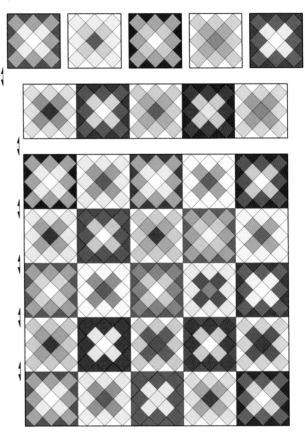

Quilt assembly

2 Sew the 12 black tone-on-tone 2" x 42" strips together with diagonal seams to make one long strip. Then measure the length of the quilt top through the center; trim and add the side borders. Measure the width of the quilt including the borders just added; trim and add the top and bottom borders. Press the seam allowances toward the borders.

3 Piece the middle border using 2¼" squares of assorted values and the black tone-on-tone 3¾" triangles. Sew triangles to the left and right sides of three squares as shown. Join these units and two additional 3¾" triangles to make a pieced strip. Square the ends of the strip by cutting ¼" beyond the point of the square, preserving the ¼" seam allowance.

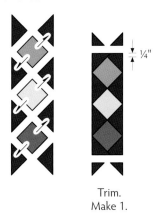

Trim.
Make 1.

4 Repeat step 3 to make four strips with four squares, three strips with five squares, and one strip with six squares.

Make 4.   Make 3.   Make 1.

5 After you complete the strips of on-point squares, sew border strips for the quilt referring to the diagram at right, adding the 3"-wide black tone-on-tone strips and 3" squares as specified. Sew the left and right side borders to the quilt first, then add the top and bottom borders. Press the seam allowances toward the inner border.

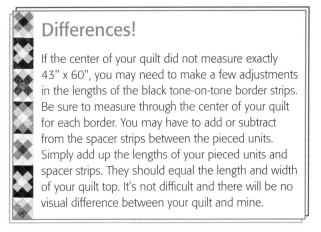

Differences!

If the center of your quilt did not measure exactly 43" x 60", you may need to make a few adjustments in the lengths of the black tone-on-tone border strips. Be sure to measure through the center of your quilt for each border. You may have to add or subtract from the spacer strips between the pieced units. Simply add up the lengths of your pieced units and spacer strips. They should equal the length and width of your quilt top. It's not difficult and there will be no visual difference between your quilt and mine.

6 Measure, cut, and sew the black tone-on-tone 2"-wide outer border to each side of the quilt. Press the seam allowances toward the outer border.

Adding borders

Finishing

For additional instructions on layering, basting, and quilting, refer to "Finishing School" on page 76. Use the black tone-on-tone 2½"-wide bias strips to make and attach the binding.

Feels Like Home

Baskets—filled with flowers, gifts, or homemade cookies—make me smile. My love of Basket blocks is apparent in this very special quilt. After I made this quilt, my friend Debbie was telling me how much she liked it. I said to her that designing this quilt "feels like home." She and I looked at each other and instantly said, "That's it! We have a name for the quilt." Come on home with me and let's enjoy some pretty baskets!

> Nobody has ever measured, even the poets,
> how much a heart can hold.
>   –Zelda Fitzgerald

Materials

Yardage is based on 42"-wide fabric.

3⅓ yards of black tone-on-tone print for sashing, setting triangles, border, and binding

2½ yards *total* of assorted medium and dark neutral prints for blocks

2½ yards *total* of assorted light neutral prints for blocks

½ yard of gray-checked wool for appliquéd vine

Scraps of cotton and wool for appliquéd leaves and berries

3½ yards of fabric for backing

62" x 72" piece of batting

⅜" bias-tape maker for basket handles

Cutting

Cutting is given for one block; the total number of blocks you'll need to cut is in parentheses.

Cutting for 1 Block A (5 total)

From 1 light print, cut:
   8 squares, 3" x 3"
   3 squares, 2½" x 2½"
   2 rectangles, 2½" x 6½"

From 1 medium or dark print, cut:
   8 squares, 3" x 3"
   1 square, 2½" x 2½"

Cutting for 1 Block B (4 total)

From 1 light print, cut:
   1 square, 8½" x 8½"; cut in half diagonally to yield
      2 triangles (1 is extra)
   2 rectangles, 3" x 5½"
   1 square, 3" x 3"
   1 square, 3⅜" x 3⅜"; cut in half diagonally to yield
      2 triangles

From the assorted medium and dark prints, cut:
   27 squares, 1¾" x 1¾"
   1 bias strip, ¾" x 12"

Cutting for 1 Block C (4 total)

From 1 medium or dark print (for basket), cut:
   1 square, 6⅞" x 6⅞"; cut in half diagonally to yield
      2 triangles (1 is extra)
   1 square, 4¼" x 4¼"; cut into quarters diagonally to yield
      4 triangles

From a second medium or dark print (for accent triangles and handle), cut:
   1 square, 3" x 3"
   1 square, 4¼" x 4¼"; cut into quarters diagonally to yield
      4 triangles (1 is extra)
   1 bias strip, ¾" x 13"

From 1 light print, cut:
   1 square, 8⅞" x 8⅞"; cut in half diagonally to yield
      2 triangles (1 is extra)
   2 rectangles, 2½" x 6½"
   1 square, 3" x 3"
   1 square, 2½" x 2½"

Cutting for 1 Block D (4 total)

From the assorted medium and dark prints, cut:
   3 squares, 2¼" x 2¼"; cut in half diagonally to yield
      6 triangles

From 1 medium or dark print (for basket bottom), cut:
   1 square, 1¾" x 1¾"
   2 squares, 2¼" x 2¼"; cut in half diagonally to yield
      4 triangles

From the assorted light prints, cut:
   4 squares, 2¼" x 2¼"; cut in half diagonally to yield
      8 triangles

From 1 light print (for background), cut:
   1 square, 1¾" x 1¾"
   2 rectangles, 1¾" x 3"
   1 square, 2¼" x 2¼"; cut in half diagonally to yield
      2 triangles

Cutting for 1 Block E (4 total)

From 1 light print, cut:
   1 square, 4¾" x 4¾"
   1 square, 2¼" x 2¼"
   2 rectangles, 1¾" x 3"
   1 square, 1¾" x 1¾"

From 1 medium or dark print, cut:
   1 square, 4¾" x 4¾"
   1 square, 2¼" x 2¼"
   1 bias strip, ¾" x 6"

Sashing, Setting Triangles, Border, and Binding

From the black tone-on-tone print, cut *on the lengthwise grain:*
   2 strips, 6½" x 55"
   2 strips, 2½" x 40"
   2 strips, 2½" x 64"

Continued on page 45.

Pieced and appliquéd by Pat Wys; quilted by Leisa Wiggley
Finished quilt: 54½" x 66½"
Finished blocks: 10" x 10" and 5" x 5"

From the remainder of the black tone-on-tone print, cut:

- 18 strips, 2½" x 10½"
- 2 strips, 2½" x 16"
- 4 squares, 9" x 9"; cut into quarters diagonally to yield 16 triangles
- 2 squares, 10" x 10"; cut in half diagonally to yield 4 triangles
- 260" of 2½"-wide bias binding

Making the Blocks

The instructions are written for making one block at a time. Be sure to measure and square up your blocks when they're complete. You will be a happy quilter when you piece the top if you do this now!

Block A

1 Pair eight dark 3" squares with light 3" squares. Draw a line diagonally from corner to corner on the wrong side of each of the light squares. Sew ¼" from the line on both sides. Cut on the drawn line and press toward the dark triangles. Make 16 half-square-triangle units; one is extra. Trim the units to 2½" square.

2 Arrange 13 of the half-square-triangle units in four rows together as shown with two light 2½" squares and a dark 2½" square. Sew the squares into rows and sew the rows together. Press.

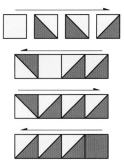

3 Sew a half-square-triangle unit from step 1 to each of the two light 2½" x 6½" rectangles as shown. Sew a light 2½" background square onto one of the rectangle units. This will create the basket "feet."

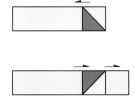

4 Sew the units from step 3 to the block unit from step 2. Press. Your block is complete. The block should measure 10½" x 10½".

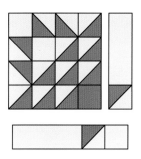
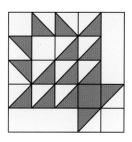

Block A.

5 Repeat steps 1–4 to make a total of five Basket A blocks.

Block B

1 Arrange and sew 21 assorted medium and dark print 1¾" squares into six rows as shown. Press the seam allowances in opposite directions from row to row.

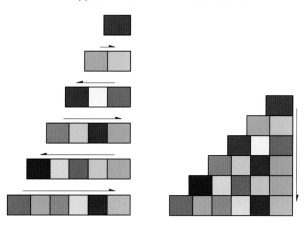

2 Trim the squares along the long side of the unit, making sure to leave a ¼" seam allowance beyond the corners of the squares.

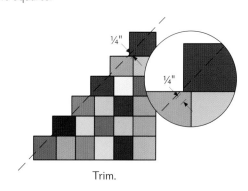

¼"

¼"

Trim.

Beware...Bias!

By trimming the squares, you've exposed the bias edges along that side of the triangle unit. Be very careful when you handle this basket base unit. It would be a good idea to do a quick line of stay stitching ⅛" from the bias edge. Don't press again until you've sewn the large triangle and its appliqué to the basket base.

3 Make bias twigs using the ¾"-wide bias strip and the bias-tape maker. Cut as desired using the photograph on page 44 as guidance for cutting and positioning the twigs. (I used one long twig for each basket, approximately 6" to 8" long, with one or two smaller branches on each.) Appliqué the twigs to the light 8½" triangle. Using the patterns on page 49, prepare and appliqué leaves and berries to the twigs as desired. Use the method of appliqué that you're comfortable with.

4 Sew the appliquéd triangle to the basket base from step 2. Press the seam allowances toward the basket.

5 Sew three medium or dark 1¾" squares together and trim the ends of the squares as you did for the basket base. Be sure to allow for the ¼" seam allowance. Make two of these units.

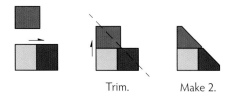

Trim.　　Make 2.

6 Sew a light 3⅜" background triangle to the diagonal edge of each unit from step 4.

7 Sew a step 6 unit to a light 3" x 5½" rectangle. Make two as shown, and then add a light 3" square to the end of one of the units.

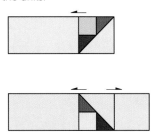

8 Sew the rectangle units to the bottom and right side of the basket base. The block should measure 10½" x 10½". Trim and square up if necessary.

Block B.

9 Repeat steps 1–8 to make a total of four Basket B blocks.

Block C

1 Make the basket accent strip by sewing four basket-fabric 4¼" triangles and three accent-fabric 4¼" triangles together as shown.

2 Make a basket handle using the ¾" x 13" bias strip and the bias-tape maker. Appliqué the handle to the light 8⅞" triangle, placing the handle about 2" in from the triangle points.

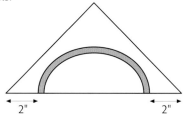

3 Sew the basket-fabric 6⅞" triangle to the accent strip. Then sew the appliquéd handle unit to the basket-base unit.

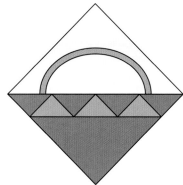

4 Make two half-square-triangle units using the light 3" square and accent-fabric square. Trim the units to 2½". Sew them to the light 2½" x 6½" rectangles as shown; add a light 2½" square to one unit as you did for blocks A and B.

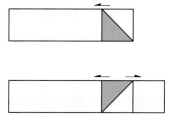

5 Sew the side units from step 4 to the bottom and right side of the basket square. Press. The block should measure 10½" x 10½".

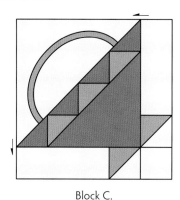

Block C.

6 Repeat steps 1–5 to make a total of four Basket C blocks.

Block D

1 Stitch the 10 light triangles with the 10 medium or dark triangles to make 10 half-square-triangle units. Trim the units to 1¾" x 1¾".

2 Arrange the half-square-triangle units together with the 1¾" square into three rows as shown. Sew the rows, and then sew the rows together. Reserve the two half-square-triangle units made of the basket fabric for the next step.

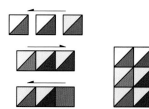

3 Make side rectangle units using the reserved half-square-triangle units, the two light 1¾" x 3" rectangles, and the light 1¾" square, as you did for the previous Basket

blocks. Add the rectangle units to the unit from step 2. The block should measure 5½" x 5½".

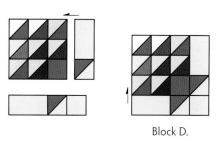

Block D.

4 Repeat steps 1–3 to make a total of four Basket D blocks.

Block E

1 Stitch together the light 4¾" square and the medium or dark 4¾" square to make two half-square-triangle units. One is extra. Square up the unit to 4¼" x 4¼". Repeat with the light 2¼" square and medium or dark 2¼" square to make two half-square-triangle units that measure 1¾" x 1¾".

2 Make a ⅜" x 6" basket handle using the medium or dark bias strip and the bias-tape maker. Insert the handle into the seam of the larger half-square-triangle unit by opening just a couple of stitches about 1" from the corner. Pin and appliqué in place. Resew the seam after you've appliquéd the handle.

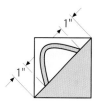

3 Make the basket feet as you did for the other Basket blocks, by sewing the two smaller half-square-triangle units to the two light 1¾" x 3" rectangles. Add a light 1¾" square to one of the units.

4 Sew the side units to the basket base. The block should measure 5½" x 5½".

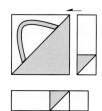 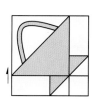

Block E.

5 Repeat steps 1–4 to make a total of four Basket E blocks.

Assembling the Quilt Top

1 Referring to the quilt assembly diagram at right, arrange the blocks, black tone-on-tone sashing strips, and setting triangles in diagonal rows. Sew the large blocks together with the 2½" x 10½" sashing strips in each row. Also sew a sashing strip to both sides of the large blocks in rows 1 and 5.

2 Sew 9" setting triangles to the small blocks as shown. Watch the placement of the triangles! These will form the sides, top, and bottom of the quilt.

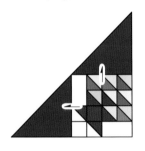 

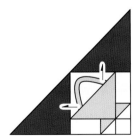 

Make 1 of each.

3 Add the small blocks from step 2 to the block rows following the assembly diagram.

4 Sew the rows together with six long sashing strips, referring to the diagram. Add the 10" corner triangles to the corners of the quilt. Press the seam allowances toward the sashing strips and toward the corner triangles. The sashing strips and triangles are cut oversized so that you can trim and square up the sides of the quilt.

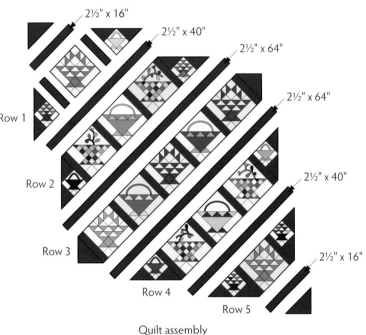

2½" x 16"
2½" x 40"
2½" x 64"
2½" x 64"
2½" x 40"
2½" x 16"
Row 1
Row 2
Row 3
Row 4
Row 5

Quilt assembly

5 Trim the quilt top so that the sides are straight and the corners are square. Be sure to trim ¼" beyond the points of the small Basket blocks.

6 Cut ½"-wide bias strips from the wool; appliqué a wool strip to a black tone-on-tone 6½" x 55" strip. Add twigs here and there as desired using the photograph on page 44 as a guide. Using the patterns on page 49, appliqué leaves and berries to the border. Feel free to use a combination of wool and cotton scraps. Vary the sizes of leaves and berries as desired. Make two appliquéd borders.

For the Love of Wool

I have fallen head over heels in love with wool and I especially enjoy mixing it with my beautiful cotton fabrics, like I did in this quilt. Some of the leaves and berries are wool; others are cotton. The vines are all made from wool. I love the speed of appliquéing with wool. I don't have to prep any fabric and turn the edges under. Oh my! There is so much more wool shopping in my future!

7 Sew the top and bottom appliquéd borders to the quilt and press.

Adding borders

Finishing

For additional instructions on layering, basting, and quilting, refer to "Finishing School" on page 76. Use the black tone-on-tone 2½"-wide bias strips to make and attach the binding.

Patterns do not include seam allowances.

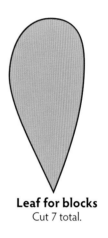

Leaf for blocks
Cut 7 total.

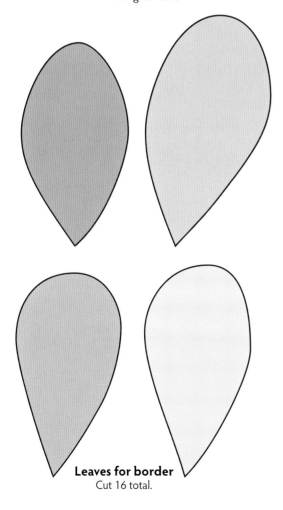

Leaves for border
Cut 16 total.

Berries for blocks and border
Cut 42 to 45 total.

Cobblestones

Sometimes it's the simplest blocks that end up making the best quilting projects. I love the cozy comfort of these Four Patch blocks, set on point in vertical rows. The addition of a linen-like background gives this project warmth and adds sophistication to the humble Four Patch blocks. Come and take a walk with me down a cobblestone path.

Why not learn to enjoy the little things—there are so many of them.

–Anonymous

Materials

Yardage is based on 42"-wide fabric.

2⅞ yards of taupe solid for setting triangles

2½ yards *total* of assorted dark, medium and light neutral prints for blocks

⅞ yard *total* of assorted fabrics for binding

3⅞ yards of fabric for backing

68" x 75" piece of batting

Cutting

From the assorted neutral prints, cut *a total of:*

196 squares, 3½" x 3½"

176 squares, 2" x 2"

From the taupe solid, cut:

8 strips, 9¾" x 42"; crosscut into 31 squares, 9¾" x 9¾". Cut into quarters diagonally to yield 124 triangles.

2 strips, 5⅛" x 42"; crosscut into 8 squares, 5⅛" x 5⅛". Cut in half diagonally to yield 16 triangles.

From the assorted binding fabrics, cut:

290" of 2½"-wide bias binding

Making the Blocks

1 Sew four assorted 3½" squares together to make a Four Patch block. See "Dispersing Seams Evenly" on page 53 to pop the seam and flatten the center of the block. Make a total of 38 blocks.

Make 38.

2 Repeat step 1 to make 44 small Four Patch blocks from assorted 2" squares.

3 Sew a Combination Four Patch block using two small blocks from step 2 and two 3½" squares. Make 22.

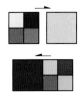

Make 22.

Assembling the Quilt Top

1 Arrange the blocks on point into seven vertical rows. There are nine blocks in rows 1, 3, 5, and 7 and eight blocks in rows 2, 4, and 6.

2 Sew taupe 9¾" triangles to the blocks as shown. Add taupe 5⅛" triangles to the rows with nine blocks as shown. Press the seam allowances toward the taupe triangles.

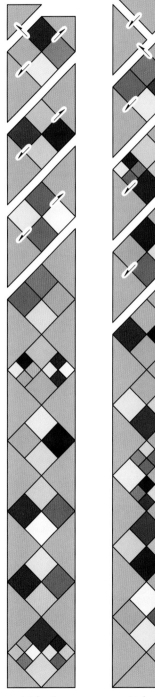

Make 4.   Make 3.

Pieced by Marty Miller; quilted by Leisa Wiggley
Finished quilt: 60" x 77"
Finished block: 6" x 6"

3 Sew the block rows together. That's it—it's as simple as can be! Your quilt top is complete.

Finishing

For additional instructions on layering, basting, and quilting, refer to "Finishing School" on page 76. Use the 2½"-wide bias strips to make and attach the scrappy binding—the perfect final touch on this scrappy quilt.

Row 1   Row 2   Row 3   Row 4   Row 5   Row 6   Row 7

Quilt assembly

Caramel Latte

Two-color quilts are always classic, and good contrast is what it's all about. This quilt makes quite a statement, combining a very subtle caramel print and a vintage-looking solid-white fabric. Whipped together, they make me think of something good to drink. The quilt construction is super easy so you'll be finished in a jiffy. Then head out and get yourself a caramel latte to sip as you enjoy your handiwork!

Materials

Yardage is based on 42"-wide fabric.

5 yards of caramel print for blocks, borders, and binding

2⅞ yards of white solid for blocks and borders

4¾ yards of fabric for backing

65" x 83" piece of batting

Cutting

From the white solid, cut:

5 strips, 4½" x 42"; crosscut into 36 squares, 4½" x 4½"

5 strips, 3½" x 42"; crosscut into 49 squares, 3½" x 3½"

5 strips, 2½" x 42"; crosscut into 72 squares, 2½" x 2½"

17 strips, 2" x 42"; crosscut into 192 squares, 2" x 2"

From the caramel print, cut:

5 strips, 4½" x 42"; crosscut into 36 squares, 4½" x 4½"

5 strips, 2½" x 42"; crosscut into 72 squares, 2½" x 2½"

17 strips, 2" x 42"; crosscut into 336 squares, 2" x 2"

18 strips, 3½" x 42"; crosscut into:

    86 squares, 3½" x 3½"

    4 rectangles, 3½" x 6½"

    14 rectangles, 3½" x 9½"

    10 rectangles, 3½" x 15½"

280" of 2½"-wide bias binding

Constructing the Units

Make all the units for the blocks and borders first. The blocks will then be a snap to put together.

1 Sew two white 2" squares and two caramel 2" squares together to make a four-patch unit. Press the seam allowances toward the caramel squares and pop the final seams as described in "Dispersing Seams Evenly" on page 53. Make 96 units.

Make 96.

2 Draw a diagonal line from corner to corner on the wrong side of the white 4½" squares. Place the squares right sides together with the caramel 4½" squares. Stitch ¼" from the drawn line on both sides. Cut on the drawn line and press the seam allowances toward the caramel print. Make 72 half-square-triangle units.

Make 72.

3 Place two half-square-triangle units right sides together with seams aligned and colors opposing one another. Draw a diagonal line from corner to corner, crossing the previously sewn seam of the half-square triangle. Stitch ¼" from the drawn line on both sides. Cut the units apart on the drawn line. Press and square up the units to 3½" x 3½". Make 72 quarter-square-triangle units.

Make 72.

The Fantastic Tucker Trimmer

I am in love with my Tucker Trimmer. I highly recommend this specialty tool. I use it for trimming both half-square-triangle units and quarter-square-triangle units. By cutting the initial pieces slightly oversized, and then trimming them down to the perfect size, you'll have absolute precision when joining units. See "The Quiltmaker's Primer" on page 74 for more information on the Tucker Trimmer.

4 Draw a diagonal line from corner to corner on the wrong side of the white 2½" squares. Pair up caramel 2½" squares and marked white squares right sides together. Stitch ¼" from the drawn line on both sides. Cut on the drawn line and press the seam allowances toward the caramel print. Make 144. Square up each unit to 2" x 2".

Make 144.

Pieced by Teresa Wade; quilted by Leisa Wiggley
Finished quilt: 57½" x 75½"
Finished block: 9" x 9"

5 Sew together two caramel 2" squares and two half-square-triangle units from step 4 as shown to make an hourglass unit. Make 72 units.

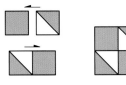

Make 72.

Making the Blocks

1 Arrange four of the four-patch units, four caramel 3½" squares, and one white 3½" square into rows as shown. Sew each row together. Press toward the caramel squares. Sew the rows together. Make 17 Chain blocks.

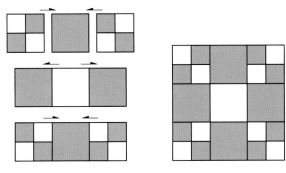

Make 17.

2 Arrange four hourglass units, four quarter-square-triangle units, and one white 3½" square in rows as shown. Sew each row together and press as indicated by the arrows. Sew the rows together and press. Make 18 Star blocks.

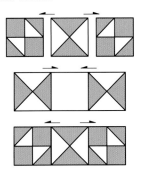
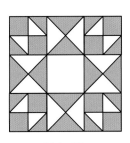

Make 18.

Assembling the Quilt Top

For quick assembly, sew the blocks together referring to "Chain Piecing Blocks" on page 75.

1 Arrange the blocks into seven rows of five blocks each. Rows 1, 3, 5, and 7 begin and end with a Star block. Rows 2, 4, and 6 begin and end with a Chain block. Sew the blocks into horizontal rows. Press the seam allowances toward the Chain blocks. Sew the rows together and press the seam allowances open.

Quilt assembly

2 Sew four-patch units, caramel 3½" squares, and caramel 3½" x 9½" spacer rectangles together as shown to make the inner-border strips. Make two of each. Sew the longer strips to the sides of the quilt. Press the seam allowances toward the border. Sew the shorter strips to the top and bottom; press.

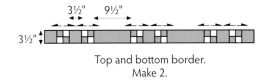

Top and bottom border.
Make 2.

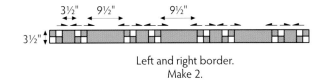

Left and right border.
Make 2.

3 Sew white 3½" squares together with caramel spacer rectangles as shown to make the outer-border strips. Make two of each.

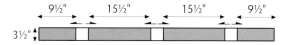

Top and bottom border.
Make 2.

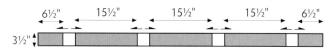

Left and right border.
Make 2.

4 Sew the longer strips to the sides of the quilt. Press the seam allowances toward the outer border. Sew the shorter strips to the top and bottom; press.

Finishing

For additional instructions on layering, basting, and quilting, refer to "Finishing School" on page 76. Use the caramel 2½"-wide bias strips to make and attach the binding.

Adding borders

Bee-U-tiful

I love incorporating linen into my quilting projects. I used it for both the background and backing of this lovely table runner. It may not be obvious, but the pieced top is appliquéd to the linen background. This runner creates a warm welcome in any home. It's long enough that it runs the length of my table with a very generous drop on the ends.

Pieced by Sarah Gafnea; quilted by Leisa Wiggley
Finished table runner: 21½" x 106½"
Finished block: 10" x 10"

Great things are done more through courage than through wisdom.

–German proverb

Materials

Yardage is based on 42"-wide fabric.

2 yards *total* of 2 or 3 light neutral linens with a small-scale checked pattern for table-runner background

1½ yards *total* of assorted medium and dark neutral prints for blocks, appliqués, and setting units

½ yard of light print for blocks

½ yard *total* of assorted light and medium neutral prints for blocks and setting units

¾ yard of fabric for binding

2½ yards of fabric for backing

27" x 112" piece of batting

Cutting

From the assorted light and medium prints, cut:

28 squares, 2½" x 2½"
28 rectangles, 2½" x 6½"

From the light print, cut:

5 strips, 2½" x 42"; crosscut into 28 rectangles, 2½" x 6½"

From the assorted medium and dark prints, cut:

195 squares, 2½" x 2½"

From the linen, cut *a total of:*

3 pieces, 21½" x 36"

From the binding fabric, cut:

270" of 2½"-wide bias binding

Making the Blocks

1 Lay out nine assorted medium and dark 2½" squares in a nine-patch formation. When you're pleased with the arrangement, sew the squares together in three rows to form the nine-patch units. Press as indicated. Sew the rows together. Make seven blocks.

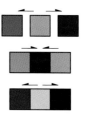

Make 7.

2 Sew light 2½" x 6½" rectangles to the left and right sides of each nine-patch unit. Press toward the nine-patch units.

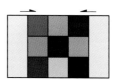

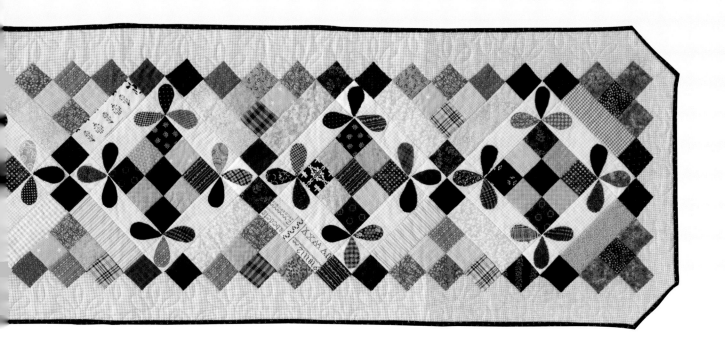

3 Sew an assorted light or medium 2½" square to each end of the remaining light 2½" x 6½" rectangles. Press the seam allowances toward the squares. Make 14.

Make 14.

4 Sew the units from step 3 to the units from step 2 to complete the blocks. Make seven.

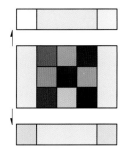 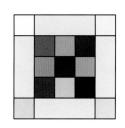

Make 7.

5 Using the pattern on page 63, cut and prepare 84 teardrop appliqué shapes for your favorite appliqué method. I used freezer paper and mixed some wool shapes in with the cotton.

6 Appliqué three teardrops in each corner to complete the Honeybee blocks.

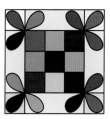

Make 7.

Making the Setting Units

1 Sew an assorted medium or dark 2½" square to each end of an assorted light or medium 2½" x 6½" rectangle. Choose squares that are darker than the rectangles. Make 16 of these units.

Make 16.

2 Sew six assorted medium or dark 2½" squares together as shown. Sew an assorted light or medium 2½" x 6½" rectangle to the long side of the 2½" squares. Make 12 units.

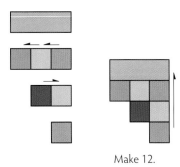

Make 12.

3 Sew an assorted medium or dark 2½" square to one end of the rectangle in the step 2 unit as shown. Press the seam allowances toward the square. Sew a step 1 unit to the side to complete the side setting unit. Make 12.

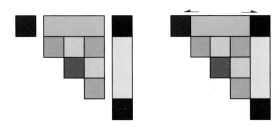

Make 12.

4 Sew four squares together as shown and add a unit from step 1 to make a corner setting unit. Make four.

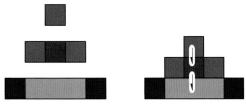

Make 4.

Assembling the Table Runner

1 Sew the side setting units to the left and right sides of the Honeybee blocks as shown. Make five of these units.

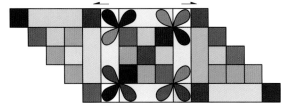

Make 5.

2 Sew a side setting unit to the remaining two Honeybee blocks as shown.

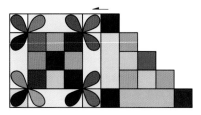

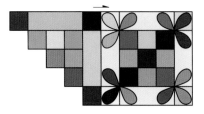

3 Sew the block and setting units together to create the center of the runner. Sew two corner setting units on each end of the runner.

4 Cut and sew the three 21½" x 36" linen pieces together to make a background that's 21½" x 107".

5 Place the center of the runner on the background. Lightly spray baste it in place, or add appliqué pins to stabilize it while stitching. Appliqué the blocks to the background by hand or machine.

Trim corners after quilting.

Quilt Before or After

In addition to the linen background, I made the backing from linen as well. Before I appliquéd it, I sent this to my dear friend Leisa, a long-arm machine quilter with amazing talent. She did a fabulous job quilting a free-motion design on the linen.

After it was quilted and returned to me, I appliquéd the center of the table runner onto the quilted base by turning the edges under and pressing them. I added a bit of fabric glue to hold them in place and machine appliquéd the entire piece onto the quilted background. I added machine quilting using monofilament and quilted in the ditch around all the squares and blocks. This firmly attached the runner to the background quilt. I was very happy with the result; however, you could certainly appliqué the pieced blocks first, and then do the quilting.

Finishing

For additional instructions on layering, basting, and quilting, refer to "Finishing School" on page 76. Before binding the runner, I cut the corners at an angle to add visual interest. Use the 2½"-wide bias strips to make and attach the binding.

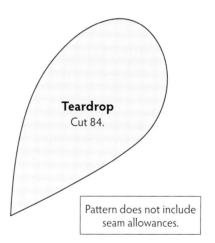

Teardrop
Cut 84.

Pattern does not include seam allowances.

La Belle Fleur

This bed runner provides an opportunity to feature a wonderful neutral background print as well as try your hand at English paper piecing. The hexagon flowers (the "beautiful flowers" that give this project its name) are really fun to make—I even made some out of wool. There are several of my favorite things in this project: flowers, fabulous fabrics (including linen and wool), appliqué, buttons, and rickrack. It doesn't get much better!

I will be the gladdest thing under the sun! I will touch a hundred flowers and not pick one.
–Edna St. Vincent Millay

Materials

Yardage is based on 42"-wide fabric.

2 yards of light print for flower-appliqué background

1½ yards *total* of assorted light, medium, and dark neutral prints for hexagon flower and leaf appliqués

⅞ yard of taupe print for sashing and binding

⅜ yard of taupe solid for stem and vine appliqués

⅓ yard of linen for leaf-and-vine-appliqué background

6 yards of ivory jumbo rickrack

2½ yards of fabric for backing

40" x 96" piece of batting

⅜" bias-tape maker for stems and vines

Buttons for embellishment (optional)

Cutting

From the linen, cut:
2 strips, 4½" x 36½"

From the taupe print, cut:
6 strips, 4½" x 36½"
76" of 2½"-wide bias binding
190" of 1½"-wide bias binding

From the taupe solid, cut:
200" of ¾"-wide bias strips

From the light print, cut:
3 rectangles, 20½" x 36½"

Making the Hexagon Flowers

1 Using the template patterns on page 68, make paper templates for the small, medium, and large hexagons. I use any heavyweight paper that I have lying around—manila folders, magazine inserts, etc. You can reuse your templates several times, so the number you need will vary. Make at least 14 of each size.

2 Lay the hexagon template on the wrong side of your fabric. Cut a ⅜" seam allowance around all sides of the hexagon template. Cut seven hexagons for each flower.

3 Pin the paper template to the fabric. You can also use a paper clip to hold the paper template in place while you sew. Baste around all sides of the hexagon by folding the seam allowance over the side of the paper. Take long stitches and make sure you anchor the fold in the fabric at each point. I sew only the fabric and don't pierce the paper. After stitching around the hexagon, cut the thread, leaving a long tail of thread at least 1". You don't need to tie a knot. Leave the paper template in place after basting. Make seven hexagons of the same size.

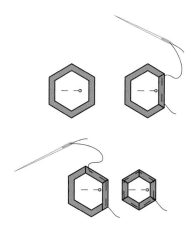

4 Whipstitch seven hexagons together along the edges to make a flower unit. Begin with the center hexagon and work your way around the center.

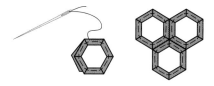

5 Press the flower unit from the right side and gently remove the hexagon papers. Leave the basting in place until after the flower is appliquéd to the background.

6 Repeat steps 2–5 to make 6 large flowers, 12 medium flowers, and 12 small flowers.

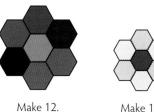

Make 12.   Make 12.

Make 6.

Pieced by Pat Wys; quilted by Leisa Wiggley
Finished bed runner: 92½" x 36"

7 Appliqué six of the small flowers onto the large flowers. This makes a terrific-looking layered flower!

Wool Is Wonderful!

I made a couple of the hexagon flowers out of felted wool. To do that, simply trace around the hexagon template, cut on the line, and whipstitch the woolly hexagons together. There's no need to add any seam allowances.

Making and Appliquéing the Bed Runner

1 Sew a linen 4½" x 36½" strip between two taupe 4½" x 36½" sashing strips. Make two of these units. They should measure 12½" x 36½".

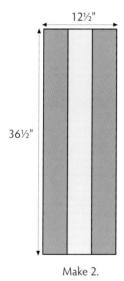

Make 2.

2 Make two 37"-long bias vines using the taupe-solid ¾"-wide bias strips and the bias-tape maker, following the package directions. Appliqué the vines to the center of the linen strip in the units from step 1.

3 Appliqué a small hexagon flower in the center of each vine.

4 Using the leaf pattern on page 68, make a template and prepare 53 leaves for appliqué using your favorite method. I used freezer-paper appliqué. Appliqué 16 leaves to each of the units from step 1.

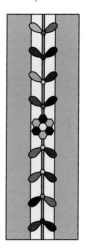

Make 2.

5 Make additional ¾" bias stems for the bouquets. Make 12 stems that are approximately 16" long for the larger bouquets. Make two that are approximately 12" long and two that are 9" long.

6 Appliqué the stems, leaves, and flowers onto the three light 20½" x 36½" rectangles. Refer to the placement guides below and the photograph on page 66.

 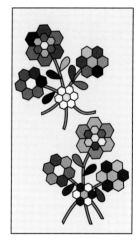

Make 1 and 1 reversed.   Make 1.

Assembling and Finishing the Bed Runner

1 Sew the appliquéd sections together with the remaining two taupe print 4½" x 36½" strips as shown.

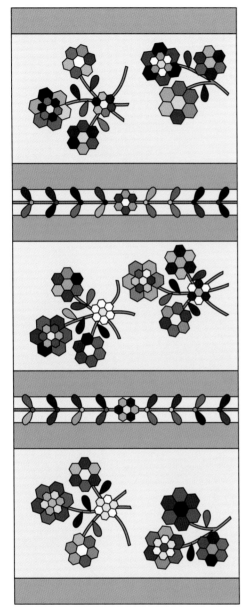

Runner assembly

2 Layer, baste, and quilt.

3 Bind the short edges of the bed runner with the taupe-print 2½"-wide bias strips.

4 Cut two lengths of rickrack to match the long edges of the bed runner. With the center of the rickrack ¼"

from the edge of the runner, machine baste it in place using a scant ¼" seam allowance.

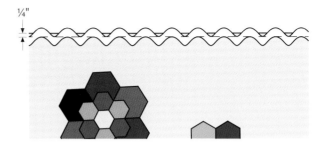

5 Align the taupe-print 1½"-wide bias strips with the raw edges of the runner's long sides. Sew them to the runner using a ¼" seam allowance and stitching through the basted rickrack and quilted runner.

6 Fold the fabric strip over to the back of the runner. Turn the raw edge under ¼" and hand stitch the binding to the back of the quilt. This will cover the row of machine stitching and one side of the rickrack. The other side of the rickrack will pop up and form a terrific decorative edge for your bed runner.

7 As an added decorative touch, I sewed buttons to each leaf intersection on the vines. I love to add special accent touches like this as the final exclamation point on my quilted piece

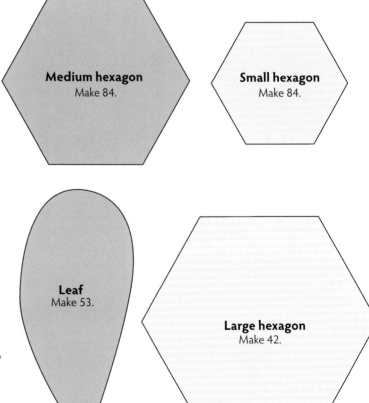

Medium hexagon
Make 84.

Small hexagon
Make 84.

Leaf
Make 53.

Large hexagon
Make 42.

Back-Porch Basket

My love of folk-art flowers with a touch of whimsy shines through in this pillow, with its mix of wool, cotton, and linen fabrics. It could take a place of honor in just about any setting—on a cozy bed or on a sofa in a screened porch—and adds a lovely accent to make you smile. If you're in the South, come visit me on my back porch. I'll be waiting with a glass of sweet tea and this great pillow!

Appliquéd and sewn by Pat Wys
Finished pillow: 36" x 18"

Materials

Yardage is based on 42"-wide fabric.

1⅛ yards of cream-checked fabric for pillow front and back

12" x 18" piece of gray-checked wool for stem and vine appliqués

6" x 15" piece of dark print for basket appliqué

5" x 16" piece of small-scale checked fabric for basket rim and bottom appliqué

Assorted cotton and wool scraps for flower and leaf appliqués

3½ yards of dark-brown jumbo rickrack

2 pillow forms, 18" x 18"

2 pieces of batting, 18½" x 36½"

Batting scraps

Heavy thread for stitching pillow forms

Buttons for embellishment (optional)

Cutting

Before you cut, sew the pillow forms together, referring to "Preparing the Pillow Form" below.

From the cream-checked fabric, cut:
2 rectangles, 18½" x 35½"*

From the gray-checked wool, cut:
76" of ½"-wide bias strips
56" of ⅜"-wide bias strips

*The rectangles should be the same length and width as the pillow form after stitching together. Remember to add ½" for seam allowances. The batting pieces should be the same size as well.

Preparing the Pillow Form

When I went looking for a rectangular pillow form that wasn't too puffy, the only ones that I found were smaller than I wanted. To make a custom-sized pillow form, I bought two 18" square pillows and stitched them together. Depending on how you assemble your pillow form, the size may be a bit different than how mine turned out. If you have square pillows that are at least 18" x 18", you can make adjustments to my directions quite easily.

1 Sew the two pillow forms together side by side to create one long pillow. Use a whipstitch and a double strand of heavy thread.

2 To smooth out the pillow forms, make a cover from the batting pieces. Stitch the batting rectangles together on three sides. If you have a deep V in the area where you stitched the pillows together, fill the area with a strip or two of batting scraps; then slip your pillow into the batting cover. Whipstitch the end closed. You have your final pillow form. Measure and use these dimensions to cut the fabric for your pillow front and back.

Appliquéing the Pillow Top

1 Using the patterns on pages 72 and 73, prepare your appliqué motifs using assorted wool and cotton scraps. Use your favorite method for appliqué. (Hand or machine appliqué—it doesn't matter. Do what makes your heart sing.)

2 Make the vines using the wool bias strips. Appliqué them first, using the narrower strips as stems for the white bellflowers. Use the diagram as a guide for placement. Add the leaves and berries, followed by most of the flowers. Sew the basket, basket rim, and basket bottom before adding the last two flowers in the foreground.

Finishing the Pillow

1 Baste the rickrack to the front of the pillow all around the edges so that the center of the rickrack is ¼" from the edge. Half the rickrack will hang over the edge of the pillow background. If you're using buttons to embellish your project, add them now.

¼"

← Baste.

2 Sew the pillow back to the pillow front with right sides together using a ¼" seam allowance. Make sure the rickrack is lying flat between the two pieces. Leave an opening on one of the long sides of the pillow to put your pillow form through.

3 Turn the pillow right side out. Press well. Insert your pillow form through the opening of the pillow cover. Turn ¼" under on the pillow front and back and whipstitch the opening closed. Your pillow is complete! (Don'cha just love it?)

Patterns do not include seam allowances.

Flower petal
Cut 6.

Flower petal
Cut 3.

Flower petal
Cut 6.

Berry
Cut 30.

Basket bottom
Cut 1.

Flip along dashed line to complete pattern.

Flower center
Cut 3.

Basket
Cut 1.

Flip along dashed line to complete pattern.

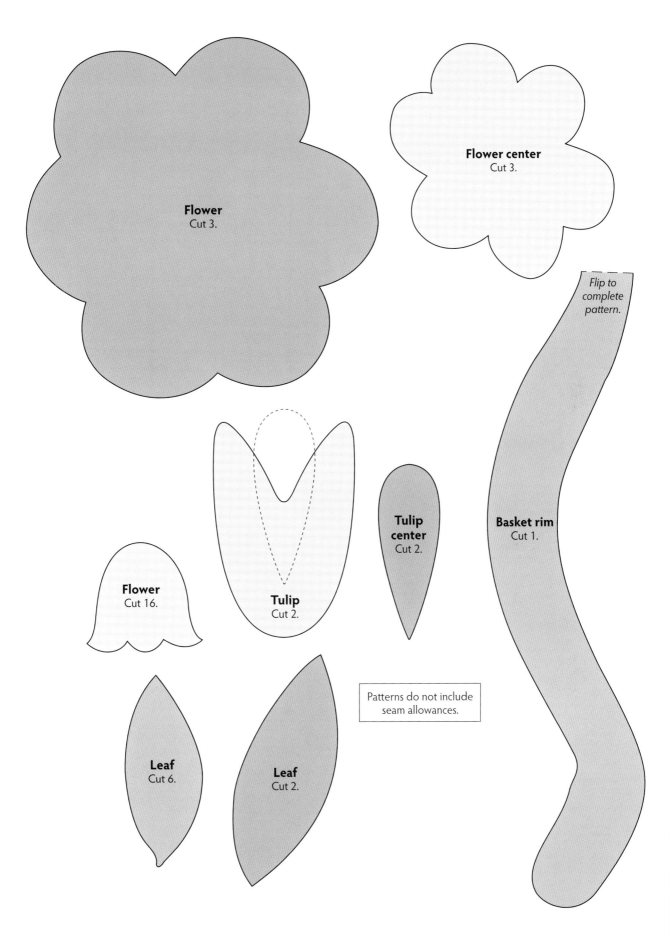

Flower
Cut 3.

Flower center
Cut 3.

Flip to complete pattern.

Flower
Cut 16.

Tulip
Cut 2.

Tulip center
Cut 2.

Basket rim
Cut 1.

Patterns do not include seam allowances.

Leaf
Cut 6.

Leaf
Cut 2.

The Quiltmaker's Primer

We ourselves feel that what we are doing is just a drop in the ocean, but the ocean would be less because of that missing drop.

–Mother Teresa

Use this primer as a reference tool and guide as you make the quilts in this book and other projects along the way. Even if you've been making quilts for years, it's good to revisit the standard techniques every now and then. You never know when you might learn something new! If you're a beginner, this section will help reinforce the techniques you're learning until they become a comfortable part of your quilting routines. Welcome to the classroom.

For information on subjects and techniques not covered here, visit ShopMartingale.com/HowtoQuilt for free, downloadable instructions.

Plan Ahead

Here is a groundbreaking piece of advice. Before you start any project, do this first: Brew yourself a cup of tea or coffee, sit down, and read the pattern! You probably think I'm being dramatic, but I'm not kidding. Read, make notes, and plan ahead. I believe that if quilters would read a pattern thoroughly and carefully *before* they start sewing, a huge percentage of mistakes in the quilting process could be avoided.

Plan which fabrics you want to use and where you want to use them. Make snippet charts and notes along the way. When you cut the pieces for a block or unit, pin together the fabrics that will be sewn together. That way you won't go wrong. Plastic ziplock bags are readily available in the grocery store and are a handy way to keep pieces organized.

If you're interrupted and have to stop working on a project before it's finished (life does that to us), mark the place in the book where you stopped, and then pin a note to the corresponding point in your sewn pieces. You can pick up easily where you left off if you take this one little step.

It's always a good idea to make a sample block from scraps first. Sample blocks help make you aware of any pitfalls you might encounter later on. And if you use light fabrics, you can use the sample block as a label for the back of the quilt.

The time you spend planning your quilt will reward you in the construction process. An organized project is a project less likely to have problems. Ask me how I know!

Prewashing Fabrics

I hope the quilt police are busy elsewhere when I make this confession: I don't always prewash my fabrics (although I know I probably should). Dye-catcher sheets available in grocery stores, special quilt-fabric detergents found in quilt

shops, and a dye-setting product called Retayne have all made it easy to skip prewashing. You can use these products to wash a quilt after it's finished without worrying about the colors bleeding, even if you didn't prewash the fabrics. I use them all and have not had any problems with bleeding. Besides, I love the wrinkly, vintage look my quilts have when they're washed after being quilted.

Tools—the Toys of the Quiltmaker

Remember the excitement of a brand-new pencil box or lunch box to take to school at the beginning of the year? You can relive those days with new quilting tools! The quilting industry introduces new tools all the time. I think it's important to learn about new tools that can make our quilting lives easier. And it's also important to remember that our ancestors made wonderful quilts by candle- or lamplight with a simple needle and thread.

I have some favorite tools that I used to make the quilts for this book. Here's the lineup and a brief description of each.

The Tucker Trimmer. Oh baby, this tool is my go-to toy. I walk around the sewing room with this thing in my hand. While any regular square ruler can be used to square up units and blocks, the Tucker Trimmer distinguishes itself from the pack in two ways. First, the tool has minimal markings and isn't busy. Measurements are easy to locate in a jiffy. The tool also includes the 45° angle in two directions, with axis points for each size. This enables me to square up quarter-square triangles with ease. Deb Tucker, designer of this tool, sings my song when she advocates slightly oversizing units when cutting and sewing. After sewing and pressing, I trim them down to the exact size with her tools. I love, love, love all of Deb's tools. They're the backbone of my sewing toolbox. (See her website for additional information: studio180design.net.)

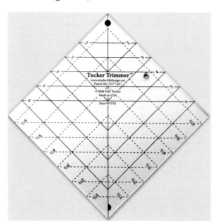

Bias-tape makers. I used to use bias bars. Since I was shown a bias-tape maker, the bias bars are no more! I have a tape maker in every size. The ones I seem to use the most are the ¼", ⅜", and ½" sizes. They're easy to use; just follow the package directions.

Fabric-glue pen. I use this all the time for basting appliqués in place. I buy refills by the truckload—I don't want to wake up in the middle of the night from a nightmare in which I ran out. They are an appliquér's best friend. Trust me on this one. Mine is a Sewline fabric-glue pen; Fons and Porter have a similar product called a Glue Marker.

Chain Piecing Blocks

Once you've arranged all of your blocks, you'll sew them together in rows. This chain-piecing technique allows you to stack all of the blocks for your quilt at one time so that you can sew the blocks and rows together without having to get up from your sewing machine. You will save so much time, keep the blocks in order, and still be able to maintain a high level of sewing precision. Your quilt can be any size with unlimited numbers of blocks. I will use a five by six block layout as an example.

1 Lay out and arrange the blocks until you're pleased with the placement. Your blocks will be arranged in horizontal rows and vertical columns. In the example, there are six rows and five columns.

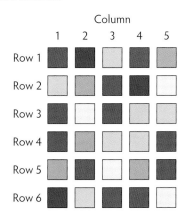

2 Flip the column 2 blocks over so that they're right sides together with the blocks in column 1. They are now in sets of two blocks each.

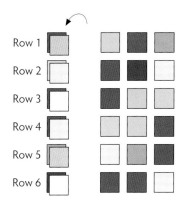

3 Stack the row 1 blocks on top of the row 2 blocks. Place these two sets on top of the row 3 set, then the rows 1, 2, and 3 blocks go on top of the row 4 set, and so on. In other words, stack the sets of two in order so that you have one pile of stacked sets.

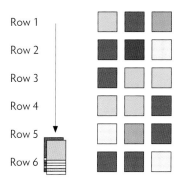

4 Stack the blocks in the same manner for columns 3–5. You'll have one stack of blocks paired right sides together and three stacks of single blocks, all right sides up.

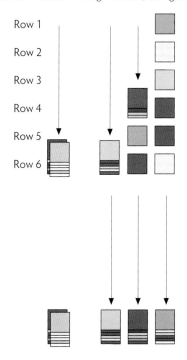

5 Pick up the first stack of paired blocks and place it on top of the stack from column 3. Place that stack on top of the column 4 stack, and then on top of the column 5 stack. You now have the whole quilt stacked in order. Put a pin in the top-right corner of the stack. This will keep the orientation of blocks correct and give you a point where you can begin sewing.

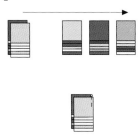

6 Time to sew. Make sure you have a full bobbin, because you won't want to run out of thread in the middle of sewing the quilt top together.

7 At your machine, pick up the first set of blocks, which are stacked right sides together, and sew them together along the right side (pinned side). This is the column 1, row 1 block and the column 2, row 1 block. Without lifting the presser foot or clipping threads, pick up the next set of blocks and sew them together along the right side. Continue chain piecing all the blocks in pairs. When you reach the last pair, remove the chain of blocks from the machine—the first two columns are nicely sewn and will be chained together forever. Open the blocks.

8 Sew the next block in your stack, right sides together along the right side of the row 1 blocks. Then add another block to each pair all the way down the column. At the end of the column go back to the top and begin the process all over again.

9 When you're finished, each row of the quilt will be sewn together and linked to the row below by thread chains. At this point, go to the ironing board and press the

seam allowances of the blocks in opposite directions from row to row, creating opposing seams.

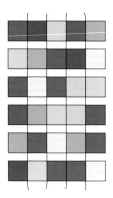

10 Back at your sewing machine, turn row 1 right sides together on top of row 2. Pin the blocks together at seam intersections and then sew the rows together. Then flip rows 1 and 2 over onto row 3 and pin and sew. Continue until all rows have been joined. **Note:** *Never* cut the chain-sewn blocks apart or you'll lose the chaining and the process won't work.

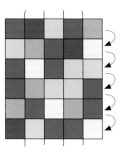

Let's Practice

Use a deck of cards to practice the stacking process. Lay the cards out and practice stacking them, pretending that they are quilt blocks. This will help you get the process embedded in your brain. Do it several times until you get the hang of it. Visit my web site, www.silverthimblequilt.com, for a tutorial. Thanks to my friend Sandy for showing me this method several years ago.

Finishing School

The choices in finishing your quilt are limitless. There's hand quilting—timeless, lovely, and oh-so-cuddly. Then we have the amazing realm of long-arm quilting. I love the beauty and intricacy of projects completed by long-arm experts. They make my work look so good, my heart stops! And, of course, there's the option of machine quilting on your sewing machine. It's so much fun to practice new skills and use all the capabilities our modern machines have to offer. Whether you choose to quilt by hand or by machine, here are a few steps of preparation to make the process easy.

1 Piece the backing with a horizontal or vertical seam to make the most efficient use of your fabric. Or, piece it with scraps, as I often do. Make sure that the backing and batting are 6" to 8" larger than the quilt top.

2 Place the backing fabric wrong side up on a flat surface. Use tape or clamps to anchor the backing so that it's taut but not stretched out of shape.

3 Place the batting over the backing, smoothing out any wrinkles.

4 Center the pressed quilt top on top of the batting and backing. Smooth out any wrinkles and make sure the quilt-top edges are parallel to the edges of the backing.

5 Starting in the center and working toward the outer edges, pin through all the layers with rustproof safety pins. Place the pins 4" to 5" apart, avoiding areas where you intend to quilt.

6 When basting is complete, remove the tape or clamps and quilt away.

Binding

I'm going to say it and I'm going to put it in print right here. I prefer bias binding in almost *every* situation. Why? For several reasons: First, for the longevity of the quilt. I believe it's more durable. Second, for the subtleness of the edges of the quilt. It's softer and drapes so well. Third, for the ease of application and construction. In my teaching workshops and lectures people often tell me that bias binding is difficult to make and takes too long. Follow these steps and you'll find it doesn't take one minute longer to cut bias binding than straight-edge binding. And, is there anything prettier than a stripe or plaid cut on the bias and used to bind your quilt?

Make a Scrappy Binding

I like to make scrappy bindings when quilts are pieced from many different fabrics. I first sew strips of leftover fabrics together to create one piece of fabric. After I create my fabric, I fold it as I do for cutting regular bias binding. This is a terrific way to finish quilts and a great way to use leftover scraps. Of course, you can also cut bias strips from scraps and piece them together as in step 6 of "Binding" on page 78.

1 Open up your fabric with the wrong side up, so that you're looking at the entire piece of fabric. You may be using a piece of fabric that's square or rectangular. Note the numbered corners.

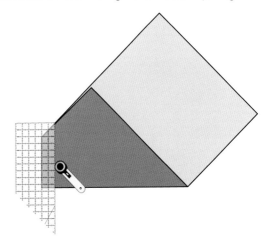

2 Fold corner 1 down to the bottom edge creating the bias fold line, which runs at a 45° angle across the fabric.

3 Fold corner 2 up to point 3, folding the bias edge onto itself.

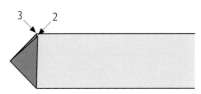

4 If you're working with a full width of fabric, you'll need to make another fold by bringing the bias point up to point 3, folding the bias edge onto itself again. (If you have less than a full width of fabric, this fold may not be necessary.)

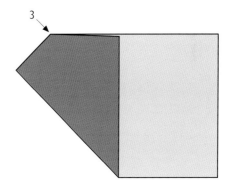

5 Rotate the fabric so that the last folded edge is closest to you. Trim off the fold, and then cut strips of the desired width. I usually cut strips 2½" wide, but you can use the width you prefer. Cut enough strips to go around the quilt, plus about 12" for mitering the corners and joining the ends.

6 With right sides together, sew the strips into one long strip, offsetting the strips by ¼" as shown. Press the seam allowances open. Fold the strip in half with wrong sides together and press.

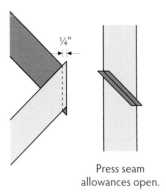

Press seam
allowances open.

7 Begin along one side of the quilt (not at a corner) and align the raw edge of the binding with the raw edge of the quilt top. Use your walking-foot attachment to sew the binding to the quilt using a ¼" seam allowance. Leave a 6" length of binding unsewn at the beginning. Sew until you're ¼" from the corner. Stop with the needle in the down position, pivot the quilt at a 45° angle, and stitch to the outer corner of the quilt.

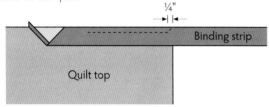

¼"

Binding strip

Quilt top

8 Clip the threads and remove the quilt from the machine. Fold the binding straight up, away from the quilt, making a 45° angle. Fold the binding back down onto itself, even with the next edge of the quilt. This is where those little angled stitches make a big difference in getting the perfect miter in the folds. Begin sewing at the fold, backstitching to secure the stitches. Stitch to the next corner and repeat the process to miter the corner.

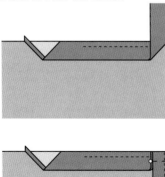

9 Stop stitching about 12" from where you began. Remove the quilt from the machine and place it on a flat surface. Fold one end of the binding back on itself, and repeat with the other end of the binding. The folds should touch each other, but should not overlap. Cut the strip on the right along the fold. Unfold the strip on the left and cut 2½" away from the fold. The length you cut should match the width that you cut your binding strips.

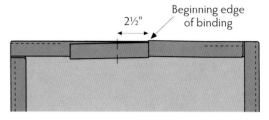

2½"

Beginning edge
of binding

Fold back end of binding even with beginning edge.
Cut 2½" from the fold.

10 Open up both ends of the binding. Place the tails right sides together so that they form a right angle. Draw a diagonal line as shown and pin.

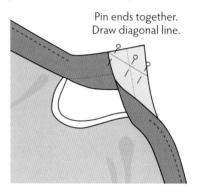

Pin ends together.
Draw diagonal line.

11 Stitch on the diagonal line. Check your stitching, making sure the binding lies perfectly flat on the quilt. Trim the seam allowances to ¼"; press the seam allowances open and refold the binding. Align the raw edges of the binding with the quilt and finish sewing the binding in place.

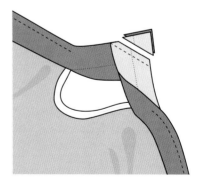

12 Fold the binding over the raw edges of the quilt to the back, so that the folded edge covers the row of machine stitching. Hand blindstitch the binding to the back of the quilt, mitering the corners.

Acknowledgments

The glory of friendship is not the outstretched hand, nor the kindly smile, nor the joy of companionship; it is the spiritual inspiration that comes to one when you discover that someone else believes in you and is willing to trust you with a friendship.

–Ralph Waldo Emerson

There are times when you receive help when you did not even realize how much you needed it. This has happened to me a thousand times during the writing of this book. I am more than a little humbled by the people in my life. I will never be able to express my love and gratitude for their love and support for me and my family. "Thank you" doesn't even cover how I feel! You all know who you are! My thanks and love are written in my heart and in the stars.

This book would never have happened had it not been for these sewing angels. (That's an understatement of epic proportion!) I love you to the moon and back, Tricia Wys, Debbie Frey, Teresa Wade, Marty Miller, Karin Efman, Sarah Gafnea, and Julie Miller. You saw a need and ran toward it. Thank you from the bottom of my heart.

To Leisa, I hope the readers of this book will notice your amazing talent. You take my quilts and make them sing! Your quilting is beyond compare. Thank you for being a huge part of this book and my life. I love you.

Thank you, Thimbles! Ten amazing years. Can't wait for the next 10! We are the club every quilter in the world should have in her sewing life. We're more than just quilts and sewing—we're family. I'm so proud of us.

Russ, we have an unbreakable bond. We have been there for each other and love is the hallmark of who we are. I love you always!

Emily and Mary Beth, oh how your mother and father love you. Thank you for your support. The quilts are yours. Later . . . much later.

To my Martingale family. I tell people everywhere what a terrific company you are and how much fun everyone is. Thank you for your support and belief in neutrals and me. You're without question a class organization. I am honored to be included in the Martingale lineup of authors.

To Ellen Pahl. Thank you so much for your meticulous editorial work. I hope you have many years of editing in your fabulous new home.

About the Author

Photograph by
Emily W. DeLoach, author's daughter

Pat has a firm belief that people are truly blessed when they have a passion for work that calls to them, challenges them, and grows with them every day. Quilting is just that for her. She's seen and felt firsthand the healing, comforting, and joyous power of quilting in the lives of many people. Pat is grateful to be a link in the chain of quilters from our past stretching toward quilters of the future.

Pat's first career was raising her family with Andy, her husband of 40 years. Teaching elementary school for over 20 years was an important part of her life as well. She began her second career as a quilt designer once her girls were in college. Teaching, lecturing, and talking about quilting with quilters every day is the highlight of her second career. Pat travels all over the country working with quilt guilds and shops. Her heart remains with her monthly club known by the nickname "Thimbles," which is celebrating its tenth year together. Pat maintains a commitment to being with them

the third weekend of every month. She says they are "the wind beneath her wings" for sure. Every day is an adventure when you choose quilting as your business.

After her first book on neutrals, Pat was left with the desire to explore them some more—so here we are. Pat will talk to anyone about the use of neutrals and the versatility of design possibilities. She's not afraid of color, though; visit her website and blog and you'll see. She loves quilts of every description and is always trying new designs and techniques.

If you're ever in the vicinity of Atlanta, Georgia, Pat invites you to get in touch, because the door is always open. You'll find Southern hospitality, sweet tea, and maybe she'll even show you her sewing room. "Ya'll come on in, let's sit and rock on the porch and talk quilts! What's better than that?"

You can find out what Pat's currently up to at her website and on her blog at www.silverthimblequilt.com.